Human Being
and Becoming

Books by David G. Benner

Presence and Encounter: The Sacramental Possibilities of Everyday Life (2014)

Spirituality and the Awakening Self: The Sacred Journey of Transformation (2012)

Soulful Spirituality: Becoming Fully Alive and Deeply Human (2011)

Opening to God: Lectio Divina and Life as Prayer (2010)

Desiring God's Will: Aligning Our Hearts with the Heart of God (2005)

The Gift of Being Yourself: The Sacred Call to Self-Discovery (2004)

Surrender to Love: Discovering the Heart of Christian Spirituality (2003)

Strategic Pastoral Counseling: A Short-Term Structured Model, 2nd ed. (2003)

Sacred Companions: The Gift of Spiritual Friendship and Direction (2002)

Free at Last: Breaking the Bondage of Guilt and Emotional Wounds (1998)

Care of Souls: Revisioning Christian Nurture and Counsel (1998)

Money Madness and Financial Freedom: The Psychology of Money Meanings and Management (1996)

Choosing the Gift of Forgiveness: How to Overcome Hurts and Brokenness, with Robert Harvey (1996)

Understanding and Facilitating Forgiveness, with Robert Harvey (1996)

Counseling as a Spiritual Process (1991)

Healing Emotional Wounds (1990)

Psychotherapy and the Spiritual Quest (1988)

Therapeutic Love: An Incarnational Interpretation of Counseling (1985)

Books Edited by David G. Benner

Spiritual Direction and the Care of Souls: A Guide to Christian Approaches and Practices, with Gary Moon (2004)

Baker Encyclopedia of Psychology and Counseling, 2nd ed., with Peter Hill (1999)

Christian Perspectives on Human Development, with LeRoy Aden and J. Harold Ellens (1992)

Counseling and the Human Predicament: A Study of Sin, Guilt, and Forgiveness, with LeRoy Aden (1989)

Psychology and Religion (1988)

Psychotherapy in Christian Perspective (1987)

Christian Counseling and Psychotherapy (1987)

Human Being and Becoming

LIVING THE ADVENTURE
OF LIFE AND LOVE

David G. Benner, PhD

BrazosPress

a division of Baker Publishing Group
Grand Rapids, Michigan

Published by Brazos Press
a division of Baker Publishing Group
P.O. Box 6287, Grand Rapids, MI 49516-6287
www.brazospress.com

Printed in the United States of America

Library of Congress Cataloging-in-Publication Data
Benner, David G.
    Human being and becoming : living the adventure of life and love / David G. Benner, PhD.
        pages cm
    Includes bibliographical references.
    ISBN 978-1-58743-379-5 (pbk.)
    1. Theological anthropology—Christianity. 2. Life—Religious aspects—Christianity. 3. Spirituality—Christianity. I. Title.
BT701.3.B45 2016
233—dc23   2015030810

16   17   18   19   20   21   22   7   6   5   4   3   2   1

To
Mark Muldoon and Larry Young

Treasured companions on the journey
who have taught me so much about
walking the spiritual path in a deeply human way
and the human path in a deeply spiritual way

Contents

Introduction

AN INVITATION TO

AN INCREDIBLE ADVENTURE

I have often joked that I must be a descendant of the great fifth-century Irish explorer and adventurer, St. Brendan the Navigator. My claim to this lineage is extremely tenuous—actually, totally fatuous. It rests on nothing more than the fact that both my parents came from Ireland (my mother emigrating from Northern Ireland with her family as a child and my father being a seventh-generation Irish-Canadian hailing from the Republic of Ireland) and that I have always had a serious case of wanderlust and an irresistible passion for exploration. I am an inveterate sailor who loves finding my way across new stretches of open sea or coastline, a seasoned hiker and nontechnical mountain climber who can't resist a new peak or trail not yet taken, and a passionate explorer of cultures and countries that are off the well-traveled tourist routes. And what is true of me in a physical sense is even truer in an intellectual and spiritual sense.

Restlessness has been my lifelong companion. My eye is always toward the horizon. I am consistently drawn to larger possibilities, driven to explore alternate perspectives, questing for bigger vistas, and addicted to hearing other voices. Those who think like me, believe as I do, or see the world in a similar way are never as interesting to me as those who offer me possibilities of encounter with alternate vantage points that are associated with their uniqueness. The journey of becoming whole and fully human has been my constant quest for sixty years, and mapping the territories of spirit and soul that are traveled on that journey has been central to my calling for the last forty of those.

But while life may feel like an adventure for me, I am quite aware that for many people it feels more like a crapshoot, a battle, or a prison sentence. Major health concerns, financial problems, or other life circumstances make mere *being* enough of a challenge that the very notion of a larger horizon of *becoming* is unimaginable. They are unable to feel the gentle tug of the evolutionary flow of life. Their preoccupation is simply to make it across the treacherous waters of an unrelenting river that sweeps them off their feet and tosses them around each time they attempt to cross it. What they long for is survival, not fullness of being.

However, many of us who are blessed to have our lower-level physiological and psychological needs reasonably met are keenly aware of the disquiet of ferment and the all-embracing ache of longing. We find it hard to settle for where we are. We feel called forward, even though it is often unclear whether we are actually moving forward or backward, up or down. Nonetheless, we are propelled by a hope that is strangely mixed with gnawing nostalgia. We feel an insatiable hunger for something we feel sure we will recognize when we taste it and a longing that resists satisfaction when we misunderstand it and seek gratification in penultimate places. We feel an instinctual draw to the horizons of further becoming; we find ourselves gazing beyond where we are as we sense the possibilities of being more than we are.

Sometimes we are seduced toward dangerous shores by the siren call of perfectionism. As we shall see, this is not only impossible to achieve but deeply soul-damaging. At other times we are tempted to give up entirely on being human and instead seek to become gods or some kind of superhumans. This is a quest that is often aided by pathological forms of spirituality that deny or minimize our bodies. But many of us want to actualize our humanity, not escape it—to be more *deeply* human, not *more* than human.

Being, Becoming, and Doing

It is these mysteries of human being and becoming that I want to explore in this book. As we shall see, becoming is a fundamental property of being. The dynamic character of being implies the tendency of everything to transcend itself. To be is to exist within an evolutionary stream that gently draws everything toward greater consciousness, expressing itself in ever-new and more complex forms.

Being human involves continuous becoming. Though infants are certainly considered human at birth, everything we know about human development demands the acknowledgment that becoming fully human is a lifelong process. It is also clear that the fullness of being human does not arise automatically with the simple passage of time. Becoming fully human is far from an automatic or inevitable outcome.

Sadly, some people treat being human as a poor excuse for their failure to live up to a higher ideal. In late 2013, the mayor of Toronto ended months of denial that he used cocaine and frequented crack houses. While remaining adamant that he had never used drugs of any sort, he conceded that if he *had* done drugs, it might have been while he was in a drunken stupor. This, he said, was something everyone should be able to understand since, like the rest of us, he was only human.

Being human is so much more than this. Second only to life itself, nothing could be a greater gift. As the pinnacle of evolutionary development, humans are entrusted with the highest levels of consciousness, complexity, intelligence, and creativity known in the universe. But with this comes an awesome responsibility. Pierre Teilhard de Chardin described humans as the arrow of evolution and the direction of its future. Not only do we have the opportunity to consciously participate in our personal and communal unfolding, but, as unbelievable as this may seem, the way in which we do so will have consequences for the continuing unfolding of the cosmos.

Everything that exists floats on a stream that flows toward transcendence. The human distinctive is not that we are part of this flow but that we possess the possibility of consciously participating in, ignoring, or even resisting it. And yet, while life is a river of change, everything that exists is being drawn toward self-transcendence and tends to conserve its own form. Paradoxically, conservation is necessary for self-transcendence. Becoming is a dance of union in which both conservation and change have a role to play, a dance in which both rest and movement are integral steps.

In humans, this dance between being and becoming involves a third dynamic: doing. Humans have a hiddenness that can be manifest only when they act in the world. Although this activity can also be a way to avoid both our being and further becoming, doing plays an indispensable role in our discovery of the hidden realms of our being and in the outworking of our becoming.

Spiritual writers sometimes suggest that doing is inferior to being. People not interested in spirituality immediately realize that this is nonsense. They often live with an elegant simplicity in which their being is their doing and their doing is their being. This is much more sensible than trying to achieve a state of being that involves an escape from doing. Even if it were possible, it is bizarre to think that it would be desirable. It just wouldn't be human. Translating our being into action is one of the ways we humans are different from rocks!

Doing is a mode of being, a particularly essential mode of being for humans. But if we are to be whole, our doing and being must be integrated. Being is the fount, and doing should be the stream that flows from it. When our doing is disconnected from the vital spring of our being, we are simply thrashing around in stagnant waters, cut off from our source. It is only when our doing is a cooperative response to the flow of the stream that emerges from the depths of our being that we can find our fullest becoming.

The Human Journey

The possibilities inherent in human becoming lead many to speak of life in terms of a journey. And what a journey it is! The self that begins the journey of human unfolding is not the one that ends it. This is particularly clear when we look not just at growth but also at the profound reorganizations of self that are involved in transformation. Authentic transformation always involves major shifts in the platform from which we experience the world, others, and ourselves. These shifts involve such dramatic change that when we notice them we often have a sense of being born again or having become a new person.

My life has been a cascading series of these sorts of reorganizations of self. I simply cannot live any other way than to open myself to the possibilities of becoming more than I am at any point in time. Of course, it is often scary to take my hands off the controls and allow myself to change in ways that I cannot regulate. But having tasted transformation, I would never trade it for the comfort of safety.

I have gone from being a dogmatic fundamentalist to a Christian who holds his beliefs with humility as I journey with those of any faith or none; from someone whose primary identification was with fellow religionists to one who now feels a profound solidarity with all humans. I cannot say that I am no longer invested in boundaries or in emphasizing uniqueness, but I can say that I am much more oriented toward similarities and connections and the sense of belonging that comes with this. Friends who have known me for a long time often comment on what they describe as my continuing reinvention of myself. I don't see it that way at all. None of the changes in me over the decades have been accomplishments, and neither are they deserving of applause. My journey is not about trading in old systems of belief or ways of being for more progressive ones. It is simply the result of my consent to the impulse of becoming that courses through my veins, inviting me to abandon my safe position on the shore of the river, jump in, and go with its flow. All that is required of me is to be open, attentive, responsive, and trusting.

Authentic transformation always changes *how* we see more than *what* we see. Most important, it involves a profound change in how we see our selves, others, and the world. Transformation begins at the boundary of what I think of as *me* and what I think of as *not-me*. Transformational changes always involve enlarging "me" and shrinking "them" or "it." It frees us from the isolation of the small, protected places of abode built by ego and introduces us to the much more expansive places of participation and belonging within larger wholes that are discovered.

The new levels of consciousness and forms of identity that emerge in these places of spaciousness and belonging build on the old ones. Transcendence always emerges out of integration, never destruction. The dynamic engine of human becoming is always love, not aggression or hostility. Attempts to kill off parts of self that we feel don't belong lead to dissociation, not wholeness. The journey of human becoming is more evolutionary than revolutionary. Transformation is movement toward transcendence through re-formation. New, higher levels of organization emerge from older ones that continue to live on within a new overall framework of self.

The human journey is a symphony of movement and rest, progress and regress, effort and consent, holding and releasing. Although it is common in Western culture to use age as a reference point for where we are in this journey, age is rather useless as a marker of progress. It is alarmingly easy to be sixty or seventy years old and still avoid the inner journey that is supposed to define the second half of life. In the same way, it is quite possible to be twenty or thirty years old and well into such second-half-of-life tasks as taming and decentering the ego in an effort to transcend it in favor of a larger self. The stages of life flow together and wash up on one another's shores in ways that make it impossible for us to know exactly what stage we are in at any point in time. But if we are honest, we will always know whether we are up on the shore watching the river or in the midst of the river's flow. And if we are reflective, we should also be able to tell whether our doing flows principally from our being and whether our being is deepening and evolving as we attend to life's invitations to further becoming.

In general terms, however, in the first stage of life becoming more than we are involves growth, whereas in the second stage of life we encounter the possibilities of genuine transformation. The English word *transformation* is a conjunction of two concepts—*trans*, or "more than," and *formation*, or "development." *Trans-formation* is "more than development." It cannot occur until *formation* has taken place, which is why it is in the second stage of life that we are most ready to engage the larger horizons of human becoming. By then, identity should be sufficiently secure as to allow us to transcend whatever has become our core sense of the self. But more important than securing identity, the crucial work of the first stage of life is the softening and decentering of ego. Ego is good at engineering self-improvement projects, but while these may change the externals of the self, they do so only by wrapping it tightly within a façade. This is not transformation. All it does is strengthen the ego as we engage in makeovers of the false self.

But regardless of your age, since you have gotten this far, chances are very good that you already know something of these possibilities of becoming in your own life. You may chronologically be in the first half of life but may be reaching into the realms of becoming that are generally associated with the second. Or you may be well into your second half of life and just beginning to sense the possibilities of awakening and transformation that were not on your radar until now.

Quite possibly, you long to move beyond the cramped quarters of your small ego-self and live out of a vastly more expansive identity and state of consciousness. Perhaps you have had moments in which you saw the world and all its inhabitants with such clarity and compassion that it felt like you were seeing through eyes transcendent to your own. Or maybe you have known the experience of loving with a love that was not your own, a love freer and fuller than you had ever experienced. Or possibly you just long to live more fully, out of a place of deep connectedness to the sacred center of everything that is, a place that is less bound by your preconceptions, history, and fears of surrender to the transcendent ground of being. These and other glimpses of the possibilities of fuller, truer, and deeper life are all extraordinarily valuable gifts because they keep us from fully accepting the so-called normal existence of the small ego-self. They keep our souls molten and our spirits questing, and they leave us more responsive to invitations of awakening in our lives.

Settling for Too Little

The American cult-classic movie *Bill & Ted's Excellent Adventure* tells the story of two slackers who move back and forth across the space-time continuum to assemble a menagerie of historical figures as their high school history project. As much as I loved it, in terms of really awesome adventures Bill and Ted settle for something far too small, something obviously more relevant to entertainment than real life. If you really want adventure, if you want to be part of something unbelievably exciting and of truly cosmic importance, there is no journey more awesome than the journey we will be exploring in this book!

How easily we settle for life in small, safe places. I know I certainly have in the past, and consequently I understand how easy it is to do. We settle for the isolation from other humans, the earth, and the Divine that comes with the restrictive filter through which we experience life from our small ego-self, yet all the while our spirits long for union with all that is. We settle for fragmentation while our spirits speak to us of possibilities of wholeness. We think we are solidly in touch with reality, but all we actually encounter are our preconceptions, thoughts, labels, and judgments about it. Taking those as reality, we then wonder why our lives seem so lacking in depth and meaning! Some might talk about transformation or expansion of consciousness, but we settle for the life we know and despair of ever experiencing anything like a profound inner awakening.

This book is for those who simply can't resist being part of the great adventure of human being and becoming. It is for those who are not prepared to stay in safe, small places, those who are aware of the call of their spirits to the expansiveness of larger places of belonging. It is for those who long for wholeness and sense that the path to it is not simply through self-improvement but involves finding our place within the larger wholes within which we exist.

It is written for seekers—Christian or non-Christian, religious or nonreligious, people of any faith or none. Finders who no longer seek will not likely be happy with what I share, no matter what they think they have found. Such people are interested in hearing only their own thoughts presented back to them and consequently listen only to voices that tell them what they think they already know. But seekers—even those of us who have tasted the possibilities I will be discussing but long for a fuller knowledge of them—live with a degree of openness and hunger that finders find intolerably threatening. This, ultimately, is what drives finders toward the certainty they crave and the aridity of their inner selves that comes along with it.

One group of seekers that has been in my mind while writing this book are those who long for larger horizons of belief and belonging but fear the cost of following the scent of freedom and spaciousness that calls them forward. If you are in this group, it is quite possible that you want to keep one foot firmly planted where you presently stand while tentatively easing the other forward. I understand this feeling. Unfortunately, you can't cross a chasm in small steps. You need to leap before you can find your feet firmly on the other side. Of course, this feels terrifying. But that is because you are focusing on your fears. When you focus instead on your longings for wholeness and allow yourself to be drawn forward by them, you will discover that the real danger lies in compromising your being and sacrificing your further becoming out of fear.

Looking Ahead

Let's pause for a moment and look ahead. I'd like to give you a preview of what follows.

In our journey together we will encounter huge concepts and vast vistas. The territory through which we will travel is what we know about human and cosmic evolution, interpreted primarily through the perspectives of the Jesuit priest and paleontologist Teilhard de Chardin[1] and the perennial wisdom tradition.[2] But don't confuse a big picture with an academic orientation. Although I draw on insights from science, philosophy, and psychology, my focus is on how these insights help us to live as humans. I will continually return to these practical implications each time I introduce scientific or philosophical findings and concepts.

Earlier chapters deal more with issues of human being, while later ones focus more on questions of human becoming. However, because being and becoming are dynamically interwoven, chapters are not organized in a linear way. The shape of how we will proceed is less a straight line and more of a continuous series of looping spirals that weave back through ideas introduced in earlier chapters in order to place them in an ever-broadening and ever-deepening context. This, I believe, is the shape of the human journey itself, and this is the way in which the totality of our being is ultimately woven together in the new forms that are manifest in our becoming.

This book includes three big themes: the wholeness of reality, the importance of the human heart, and love as the foundation of all being and becoming. We will touch on these themes repeatedly as the discussion spirals back and forth between cosmic and human being and becoming.

Ultimately, nothing is understandable unless approached from a holistic perspective. Nothing about humans is, therefore, understandable without placing humans within their natural contexts, and these are always the larger wholes within which individuals are but a part. It is only when we start with the largest wholes that we can see how smaller wholes fit within them. Understanding the way in which reality is structured like a series of nesting Russian dolls has profoundly important consequences for those who seek wholeness. Wholeness can never be experienced unless we find our place within the larger wholes within which we exist. Finding our place within those larger wholes provides us with the sense of calling and belonging that we need for full and deep human being and becoming.

The second big theme we will explore is the nature and importance of the heart as an organ of perception and source of wisdom. The heart that we will focus on is not primarily the pump in our chests but the metaphorical organ that plays such a crucial role in living out of the depths and fullness of our humanity.

"Heartfulness" complements rather than competes or interferes with mindfulness; ultimately, the only way to move beyond the egoic mind with all its pettiness and smallness is to ground the mind in the heart. When heart and mind are aligned, the heart can become the magnetic center and orienting compass that is essential for human unfolding.

The third overall theme of this book is the deep and fundamental way in which love is the foundation of all being and becoming. But the love that I describe is not the soft, sentimental love of Hollywood or Hallmark cards. Love is the word some cosmologists are bold enough to use to describe the attractional force that holds planets in orbit and provides the glue that holds atoms together.[3] It is the strongest force in the universe, but it is also the gentlest. Only love can soften a hard heart. And only love can renew trust after it has been shattered. Only love can inspire acts of genuine self-sacrifice. Only love can free us from the tyrannizing effects of fear. And only love can transform persons. Love holds all things together and grounds all being and becoming.

Meeting Your Guide

Before we launch on the journey that is ahead of us, perhaps I should say something more about myself. First and foremost, I write this book as a human. That, much more than my professional background or spiritual tradition, is the foundation of my identity. I have long been convinced that if I don't embrace this foundation fully, any other identity will be shallow, superficial, and ungrounded.

The people to whom I have always been most attracted have been profoundly human. They have been passionate seekers of further becoming. I connect with them in deep places. Their being speaks to mine and calls me to deeper and fuller levels of becoming. The presence of these people has always been luminous to me, and that luminosity comes from being—not beliefs, ego, or impression management. Borrowing from the second-century Christian theologian St. Irenaeus, I would say that nothing more honors our being, or Being itself, than humans who are fully alive.[4] My longing to be that sort of person has been an orienting compass on a pedestal at the center of my soul.

But I also write out of other levels of my being. I write as a clinical psychologist who tends to see people in terms of their barriers to awakening and further unfolding rather than in terms of their psychopathology. My professional training and practice have been within the depth psychology tradition that was first mapped by Sigmund Freud and Carl Jung. This is a psychology that focuses on the soul, not just symptoms. It is a psychology, therefore, that is uniquely sympathetic to spirituality.

Perhaps more surprising for a psychologist, the mystics have also had a very important influence on my understanding of human being and becoming. Because mysticism is rooted in humanity, they have much to offer anyone interested in developing a spiritual psychology. Mystics start with human longings and follow them to their transcendent source. They help us realize that personhood is ultimately only intelligible within a transcendent context in which we exist as partial wholes within larger wholes. By showing us what it means to be connected to the ground of human being, they help us realize the possibilities of human becoming.

The mystics have also profoundly shaped my spirituality. While I draw deeply from the perennial wisdom tradition and have benefited immensely from interfaith dialogue (particularly with Buddhists, Taoists, and Muslims), I live out my spiritual journey as a Christian. Here my tribe is Anglican, and my specific lineage is the contemplative tradition. This explains the Christian perspective that will be evident in what follows. I haven't sought to exclude it in my attempt to write primarily from the perspective of a human being. When I speak both from my own tradition and out of the depths of my humanity (not merely my religious experience and beliefs), seekers from other traditions are then able to connect to what I am describing. I know this because the same is true for me.

Candidly, I share much more common ground with secular humanists, who seek to live fully and deeply all that it means to be human than I do with religionists of any persuasion who use spirituality as a form of escape from their humanity. I also have more in common with spiritual seekers of any tradition (or none) than with spiritual finders within my own tradition. It is this common ground out of which I will speak in what follows.

And so, let the journey begin! It is a journey toward the fulfillment of our humanity. It is a journey of participation in the great cosmic evolutionary adventure. It is a journey that is deeply spiritual because it involves a return to our Source. It is the most important and most awesome journey any of us can ever make!

Lima, Peru
March 2014

1

Being Human

To be human is to live in a world of form at the border of the world of the formless. It is to experience the power of thought but sense the possibilities of awareness. It is to exist within the realm of appearance and yet have occasional glimpses of presence. It is to know the effort of doing and long for the existence of simple being.

As far as we can tell, no other form of being involves the complications and tensions that humans experience as a result of living in these borderland places. There is no reason to believe that clouds wonder whether they should let go of the rain they hold or worry about how they look as they move across the sky. Neither is there any reason to suspect that waves get tired of rolling up on beaches only to be pushed back again by the sand and rocks. There is nothing that would suggest that the sun debates whether it wants to rise in the morning or that shadows wish they could again feel the warmth of the sun when it does.

Life is simpler for other forms of being. They just do what they are. And they just are what they do. Rocks are hard, and water is movement. Except when we pay attention to it, breath flows in and out with a fluidity and naturalness that we humans seldom know in anything we do. And trees show no sign of questioning where they stand.

Only humans seem to get lost in wondering about other possible ways of being and doing. Choices are the ground of our great freedom, but they also can lead us into a great bog of quicksand. The more we thrash about in the possibilities and choices that confront us, the deeper our entrapment becomes. This is the price we pay for consciousness.

The Gift of Consciousness

While consciousness has associated costs and complications, it is unquestionably one of our greatest gifts. Without it we could never make sense of the experiences of our lives and would be destined to simply live in reaction to the events that happen to us. Without consciousness, we would not have meaningfully organized perceptions, only scattered sensations. Without consciousness, we would drift through life awash in stimulation and bereft of the most distinctive human resources for rising above the instinctual programming that was bequeathed to us by our evolutionary past.

Without consciousness, we would never know the self-transcending rapture of being drawn beyond our selves by great music, literature, or art. Neither would we know the ecstasy of orgasm, the satisfaction of a great meal, the wonder of a starry sky, the joy of rich conversation with dear friends, or the fulfillment of projects carefully planned and accomplished. Without consciousness, we could never reflect on our lives, be absorbed by something that caught our attention, or be fully present to others or ourselves. Without consciousness, we would be like rocks and trees—we would simply be what we do and do what we are. But wait a moment. Perhaps the notion of simply being what we do and doing what we are is beginning to sound alarmingly familiar!

How easily we humans allow this great gift of consciousness to slip through our fingers. How much of our lives are lived on autopilot, without awareness. I know that from experience. Although I write and talk about presence, when I look back on recent moments in any typical day, it is painfully easy to see how quickly I am drawn back into self-absorption. I get wrapped up in my thoughts, my writing, and my preferred obsessions. Each time I do this, I slip out of full consciousness and into a state of mindlessness.

Falling out of consciousness may be the core of human dysfunction. We go through our days as sleepwalkers. We may awaken for brief moments of intense emotional experience, but then we quickly blunder back into a tangled dream of preoccupation and oblivion. Most of the time we live like mindless robots. The invitation to embrace the fullness of being human is an invitation to awaken, to respond rather than simply react. It is an invitation to become full participants in our own lives. It is an invitation to climb back up out of unconsciousness each time we stumble into it. It is an invitation to reclaim our heritage as mindful beings who are wide awake and present to ourselves, others, and the world around us.

Psychology has often shown more interest in the unconscious than consciousness. But the longer I work with the unconscious, the more I come to feel that without better appreciation of its twin—consciousness—we can never really understand the mystery of persons. What we need for fully orbed human functioning is a partnership between these two dimensions of our inner lives. But fullness of consciousness does not merely come from an alliance with the unconscious. It also comes from a simpler but surprisingly powerful source: the practice of presence and learning to pay attention.

Each time we notice something we stand at the threshold of a possible awakening. Even if we notice only for a moment and then drift back into our mindless stupor, any awakening to the present moment deepens consciousness and heightens our presence. Paying attention to anything is a first step toward leaving our minds and coming to our senses. Because presence to anything is a doorway to the transcendent, it is the first step toward awakening.

Perhaps you, like me, understand the tendency to get lost in thoughts. Or perhaps the quicksand at the edges of your consciousness is made up of your feelings. Both thoughts and feelings are important, but both can make us oblivious to what is happening in our bodies and external environments. Our inner mental and emotional experiences keep us preoccupied and block us from genuine awareness.

The cultivation of awareness and presence is the single most important route to increased consciousness. Practicing awareness is learning how to be present to our lives rather than unconsciously flowing down the stream of life. In any of its forms, awareness is the essence of meditation.

Notice what changes when you name your thoughts or feelings rather than spinning or massaging them. Say to yourself, "Now I am thinking about . . ." or "Now I am feeling . . ." As soon as you do so, you will likely notice some distance from your thoughts and feelings. Possibly for the first time in your life you will notice that they are nothing more than things that pass through your mind as they float down the stream of your consciousness. They are not you. Neither do they have any concrete reality or absolute truth. You can hold them or release them. But for now, just notice them. This is being aware. Mindfulness isn't eliminating thoughts and feelings. It is being aware of your experience and then releasing it.

Awareness and the fuller levels of consciousness that it ushers in are within our reach, even if they are also beyond our grasp. Like all of the most precious aspects of being human, awareness is ephemeral. It is beyond control but accessible through gentleness and openness. It demands, however, that we pause in our doing and reconnect with our being and our essential nature.

The Nature of Being

The ground of being human is being. But what does it mean to be? While that question certainly sounds esoteric and academic (which I promised this book would not be), I am convinced you will see its relevance to being human.

The nature of being—or, put another way, the nature of existence—has long been of central interest to the world's religions. Although they differ from one another in important ways, their common teachings have long been recognized. The most obvious example of this common core is the ethical priority of loving others as our own self.[1] But the shared core of teachings is much broader and has often been described as *sophia perennis*, or the perennial wisdom tradition.[2] With only small differences, these core understandings of ultimate reality can be found in all major religions. They have, however, more often been taught by the mystics than by the dogmatists. Because the mystics of all traditions tend to be marginalized and much less influential than the dogmatists, most religious adherents know little of their own mystical tradition, never mind the large common ground it shares with other traditions.

The perennial wisdom tradition summarizes the essential nature of being in terms of what it calls the "three transcendentals"—that is, three properties of everything that exists. Those properties are oneness, truth, and goodness.[3]

To say that everything that has being is characterized by oneness is to note that naked being is always singular. Every being is necessarily one, otherwise it would not be a being but rather several beings. But everything that is exists within a web of interconnections, each thing being both a whole and a part of a larger whole. This is the web of oneness. And the foundation of this web of oneness is truth and goodness.

I recently returned from a visit to an Amerindian village in the Amazon rain forest. There I was reminded how deeply grounded

the aboriginal peoples of the world are in the perennial wisdom
tradition and these three transcendentals. Traveling with a local
guide, we were greeted by a spirited old woman who, we were
told, was the oldest person in the community and one of the last
speakers of their native language. She addressed us in Cocama as
a younger woman translated her words into Spanish and my wife
translated this into English for me. She greeted us as her brothers
and sisters and told us how happy she was to welcome us under the
canopy of the rain forest, where her people had made their home
on the edge of the river for thousands of years. She said that the
river and the rain forest had always given them everything they
needed—even though they didn't have money, they had everything
that they required to be happy. She spoke of the beauty of life in the
forest and told us that it and the river taught her people everything
they needed to know to live wisely and well. The most important
thing they taught, she said, is that everything is interconnected.
She said that if we didn't know that, maybe the visit to her community could help us to learn that it was true.

I was astounded. Right in the midst of writing this chapter,
I was with people who knew the truths I was talking about but
am still trying to learn. I was (as I always am, whenever I am
in the presence of indigenous people) humbled and exhilarated.
For these people, integral oneness is part of goodness and truth.
They are so right. Where there is truth, there is also oneness and
goodness. And where there is integral oneness, there will also be
goodness and truth.

Being, therefore, is good, never bad. It is also grounded in truth,
not falsity. And it is one—integrally whole, not a set of isolated,
independent parts. When the one, the true, and the good operate
in harmony, the result is beauty.

Christians who are used to thinking in terms of original sin
might be troubled by the suggestion that the fundamental nature
of being is essentially good. If so, they will be even more disturbed
by any suggestion that the essential nature of human being is good.

But five times in a row, the Genesis creation story reports God declaring creation to be good. And in case any doubt remains, God speaks a final time, declaring that it is all *very* good.[4]

It is a great tragedy that we have turned such good news into bad news. Missing original blessing, the church has instead often seen only original sin. Reminding us of what we have lost in doing this, Richard Rohr summarizes the good news of creation: "If you were connected inherently with the nature of Being, you would always be united and uniting, you would always do the inherently true thing, and you would always do the morally good thing. This is your deepest nature."[5] This, in a nutshell, is the implication of the nature of being for human being and becoming.

Human Nature

Many people have no trouble embracing the fact that their deepest nature is gloriously good. Secular humanists understand this truth, as do New Age religionists, Jews, and Muslims—none of whom have anything like a theology of original sin. Eastern Orthodox and Celtic Christians have also never held a theology of the essential sinfulness of humans as part of their beliefs. Other Christian traditions, however, consider belief in the depravity of humans to be a cornerstone of orthodoxy. Unfortunately, this has led many to mistrust their bodies, emotions, sexuality, intuitions, and much more. This basic mistrust then easily spills over onto others—even onto the natural world. In short, it leaves people cut off from their deepest selves and misaligned with the flow of life.

This is certainly part of the reason so many people seem to feel that being human is a pitifully poor second best to being a god. But the god they have as their reference point is not the God we meet in Jesus—that is, Jesus as he was, not as he has been shrouded by dogma. How tragic that Christians so often miss the fact that Jesus was fully human. They are so uncomfortable

Nor does CATHOLICISM

with his humanity that many feel they have to deny his sexuality. They may speak of Jesus as being fully human, but they quickly rush to add that he was also fully divine; they can't tolerate the tension between these two realities. It really shouldn't be a surprise that they lack a model of what being fully human looks like and often use the fact of their being human as an excuse for failure.

I find it ironic that my non-Christian friends are much more likely than my Christian ones to see Jesus as an astoundingly helpful example of what it means to be an enlightened, aligned, integrated, and whole human being. Unfortunately, the popular Christian image of Jesus has too much transcendence and too little humanity to be helpful in knowing how to be fully and deeply human. What a shame this is, since Christianity so clearly informs us that unless God comes to us as and where we are as humans, we can never know that we are already in God and God is in us.

But it isn't just those who believe that human nature is fundamentally sinful who use the fact of being human as an excuse for failure to live up to higher ideas. From time to time most of us have done the same—even if we have only muttered the words to ourselves as a way to excuse something we were shocked to find we had done. It is an excuse with a hidden reference point, an ideal standard that is hopelessly unrealistic for humans.

I recall a monk once telling me that the most common question people asked when he left the monastery wearing his habit was what monks do with their time. "Surely," the question seemed to imply, "you can't spend it all just praying!" His answer, he said, was always the same. "We fall down, then we get back up, then we fall down again, then we get back up again, then . . ."

I am certainly not a monk, but this is my story too. This is why long ago I gave up on spiritual self-improvement projects. If you are honest and have been paying attention to your life, I suspect this is your story as well. Whatever else this being human involves,

*what is the theology of,
"I'm only human"?

failure to live up to our own ideals and spiritual aspirations is certainly part of the picture.

Perfection and Wholeness

Given our limited experience with anything even remotely approximating perfection, the fact that humans carry within themselves a notion of the perfect is a bit of a mystery. Yet children who have known only abuse still long for a perfect parent, and lovers who have known only betrayal and disappointment still dream of the perfect partner.

As the best observers of human nature know well, very few people are as they appear. Well-constructed public masks obscure fatal flaws and parts of self that are often massively discordant with appearances. This is, of course, what makes people both interesting and incredibly frustrating.

And yet many people find it enormously hard to tame their ideals of perfection. Life is oriented around achieving or maintaining the perfect weight or body, the perfect image, or the perfect family. The paradoxical nature of perfectionism becomes clear when we realize that all of these so-called perfections are illusions. Bodies age, images never tell the whole story, and perfect families are social fabrications. The perfection we are tempted to pursue is utterly unattainable.

However, what we fail to achieve for ourselves we easily project onto others by means of idealization. We may realize that that those we idealize are not perfect, but we see them through rose-tinted glasses that seriously distort reality.

Ultimately, idealization only serves to preserve our illusions. Sigmund Freud, who gave us the first systematic understanding of idealization, was himself caught up in a lifelong idealization of his mother. Failing to see her as she truly was meant that both his psychology of women and his lifelong relationships with them were fatally flawed. Anything that compromises our ability to see things as they truly are reduces our capacity to engage life in a vital, integral, and healthy manner.

Hero worship always involves idealization. We see this in the fact that we are enormously resistant to knowing the truth of those we idealize. But a close look at the lives of any of the most widely respected people reveals that none of them has been or is perfect. As Nelson Mandela said to President Obama while discussing the weight of the mantle that the world had placed on him, "Don't consider me a saint unless you consider a saint nothing more than a sinner who keeps trying."[6]

Consistency and perfection are both seriously overrated. In art and life, beauty is often woven into flaws. As Leonard Cohen says in his song "Anthem": "Ring the bells that still can ring / Forget your perfect offering / There's a crack, a crack, in everything / That's how the light gets in."[7]

I am told that each authentic Navajo rug always has one very visible and intentional imperfection woven into it. Within Navajo spirituality, this is precisely the point where spirit moves in and out of the rug.[8] The visible flaw is the locus of the invisible spirit. Just as in Cohen's lyrics, the light comes in through the crack. Perfection is not the elimination of imperfection but the ability to recognize, forgive, and include it.[9] Only when we accept the wounds, brokenness, and imperfections can we then discover the wholeness that comes with their inclusion.

Inconsistencies, imperfections, and failures to live up to ideals are all part of what it means to be human. What seems to distinguish those who are the most deeply and wholly human is less their perfection than their courage to accept their imperfections. Accepting themselves as they are, they then become free to become more than they presently are. They then become able to accept others as they are.

The richness of being human lies precisely in our lack of perfection. This is the source of so much of our longing, and out of that longing emerges so much creativity, beauty, and goodness. It really is the cracks that let the light in. Once these cracks and flaws are embraced and accepted as part of our self, then and only then can the light flow through them out into the lives of others and into the world. This was what Henri Nouwen is referring to when he speaks of the "wounded healer" as one who mediates healing, not in spite of personal wounds but precisely because of them.[10] Our humanity, not our pseudoperfection, allows us to both receive and pass on what Christians call grace, the goodness that flows into our lives from beyond.

Spare me perfection. Give me instead the wholeness that comes from embracing the full reality of who I am, just as I am. Paradoxically, it is this whole self that is most perfect. As it turns out, wholeness, not perfection, is the route to the actualization of our deepest humanity.

Head and Heart

One of the ways in which we limit our wholeness is by overvaluing rationality. Often we seem to assume that the ideal human is someone like Star Trek's Mr. Spock, someone whose mental processes are never clouded by emotions or nonrational mental functions such as intuition or imagination. We tend to equate the mind with reason, and we are surprised when people do things that seem unreasonable. We assume that the perfect person should behave in a manner that is consistently logical and reasonable.

Think of how often you have heard people express shock when others behave in a way that strikes them as irrational—smoking in spite of the well-publicized health risks, throwing oneself in front of an oncoming bus to save a stray dog, or losing all of one's life savings through a risky financial gamble. "What was he thinking?" they might ask, or "Where did she leave her head?"

We begin to get an answer to these questions when we notice that irrationality is almost always a judgment we make of others, not of ourselves. When it comes to us, we can usually identify reasons for what we do. From a personal perspective, what we do usually feels reasonable, even if we are aware of risks that are involved. In other words, we can rationalize our behavior. By definition, however, rationalization is offering reasons for behavior that are plausible but not real. They are excuses, not the actual reasons we have done what we have done. Of course, we can never fully know why we have done what we have done; motivation is far more complex than what even the most self-aware and honest of us realize. But all of this is merely another way to say that the actual reasons behind human behavior almost always involve factors and considerations that are not simply rational and often not even conscious.

The unconscious has its own logic, but it is quite different from the logic of consciousness. While reason is a faculty of the conscious mind, the human mind involves many other faculties, many of them with roots deep in the unconscious; we live a very truncated existence if we listen only to the standards of reason. When we begin to recognize and honor these other ways of knowing and choosing, it becomes clear that "nonrational" does not necessarily mean "irrational"!

Let me give a personal example. Recently my wife and I moved from Victoria, a picture-perfect city that just happens to have the best climate in Canada, to Toronto, a large city with the extremes of Canadian weather and all the problems of a major metropolitan center. It was a fairly major move, since we were both approaching retirement and would be leaving a community with well-established friendships and moving to one in which we knew only one couple we met on a trip to arrange housing. Although we had been wondering about this move for quite a while, most of our friends heard of it only once a decision was made and the move was imminent. Not surprisingly, they wanted to know why we were moving, hoping to hear things that might make the decision more reasonable than it seemed. But although we had considered the implications of the move seriously for a number of months, it was not made on the basis of reason. If we had listened only to reason, we would have stayed where we were. At best, the pros and cons of the move canceled each other out and, at worst, definitely favored staying.

So why did we move? We moved for reasons of the heart. Quite simply, we both had a strong sense that it was the right move for us because of the way considerations of staying or moving played out in our depths. We felt peace and vitality when we thought of moving and a sense of sadness when we assumed we would stay where we were. Reflecting on this—that is, bringing the mind down into the heart—we noticed that staying seemed like it would be the result of a lack of courage and appropriate risk taking. It felt like playing life too safely, living too small. While we recognized that these feelings were not rational, we were also convinced that they were not irrational. Since the move, our belief that listening to our hearts was the right way to make that decision has only increased.

The wisdom tradition places a great deal of emphasis on learning to know, choose, and live from the heart.[11] But the heart it refers to, and the one I refer to when I use the term, is not reducible to feelings. The heart is the fullness of the mind. This is expressed in the movement beyond rationality that includes other ways of accessing wisdom.

The mind is much more than reason. It also includes subtle, generally unused and underdeveloped faculties such as intuition, imagination, symbol formation and manipulation, extrasensory perception, attention to our bodies, and attention to our deep emotions, moods, and shifting ego states. All of these factors can play an important role in life if we are prepared to move beyond rational thought as the primary instrument of knowing and deciding. All of them move us into a realm that is not *less* than rational but *more* than rational. They are, therefore, *transrational.* They include reason but also transcend it.

Humans may be hardwired for reason, but it is equally clear that we are also hardwired for many other forms of knowing and choosing. What a shame when we limit ourselves to the restrictive framework of reason. Life lived exclusively by the principles of reason is far from an expression of human perfection. It is living with one hand tied behind our back. It is living from a place that is too small and too safe. Living from the heart doesn't simply complement the mind, as if it is necessary to swing back and forth from mind to heart in order to include considerations of both. Life lived from the heart is life lived from the fullness of our being.

Anxiety, Control, and Surrender

The payoffs for living life from that small and safe place are, how-ever, huge. Even though there may also be related costs, many people count it simply too risky—sometimes even too terrify-ing—to consider anything that might move them out of their personal safety zones.

The most important of these payoffs are the ways in which living small and safe help us to manage the anxiety of living. By this I do not mean the clinical forms of anxiety that can be so crippling to those who suffer from diagnosable anxiety disorders. Clinical levels of anxiety cannot be managed by living small, although they may well drive people to try to do so. But underlying these anxieties, and common to everyone, is a lower-level form of anxiety that is simply part of the human condition. This existential anxiety is the fundamental dis-ease of being human. Usually it lurks at the edge of consciousness, only coming into the full light of aware-ness with the sort of attentiveness that comes from the practice of meditation or intentional presence. But it is always there, lurking in the background. If you feel this is not true for you, it simply means that you have been more successful than is good for you in avoiding solitude and inner attentiveness.

The roots of this existential level of anxiety sink into two, deep dimensions of human existence. The first is the essential freedom of being human. Most of the time we are oblivious to the stunning array of choices that we face moment by moment. We may feel like victims of our history and present life circumstances, and while these conditions can certainly reduce freedom, being human involves the availability of significant freedom of choice at any point in life. Things may happen to us, but we always have the choice of how we will respond to them. This, much more than what happens to us, makes us who we are. And every time we chose to avoid the anxiety caused by our freedom, we reduce that freedom—not just in the moment but also in the future.

This is how addictions work. Our real addiction is not to things like alcohol, drugs, work, or sex but to control. Addictions are strategies to avoid human vulnerability and risk. The bondage of addiction seems like a small price to pay for the apparent decrease of anxiety and freedom that comes with living life fully alive, fully awake, and fully aware. The primary function of any addiction is therefore numbing and desensitizing—it keeps us asleep and unaware. The terrors we are trying to avoid when we feed addictions are the terrors of real living in the face of the unavoidable mystery of being human. It is this terror that we most want to control and from which we most want to escape. The demon in the dark of our inner basement is nothing more or less than our fear of being fully human.

What we are most deeply addicted to is trying to escape the limitations of being human by playing God. We are all addicts because we all know the temptation to try to *be* God rather than simply being *like* God.[12] This is the religious core of addiction and the cradle of the human lust for control.

But there is a second source of the existential anxiety that we seek to control and avoid. It is what Ken Wilber calls the "optical illusion of the separate self."[13] Even though, as we shall see in the next chapter, humans exist within a thick web of interconnectedness—which can be unrecognized but not escaped—the pain of what we perceive to be our existential aloneness forms the basic wound of being human. It is the deepest level of our dis-ease.

While we cannot eliminate this underlying distressing sense of cosmic aloneness, we can minimize awareness of it. This is what we do when we build and maintain safety systems to keep life predictable and small. Avoiding risks does nothing to overcome our existential isolation and disconnectedness but rather gives a sense of no longer being helpless and vulnerable. It responds to one illusion—the optical illusion of the sense of the separate self—with another, the illusion of being in control of life with all its fragility and vulnerability.

Ultimately, control only cuts us off from the flow of life. But it is only by allowing ourselves to wade into the stream of life and be carried along by it that we can fully participate in the flow and draw on its vitalizing energy.

I have experienced the zest that can come from living in this open way, and yet I still fall back on ridiculous strategies in an attempt to control my life. For example, I exercise absurd levels of control over people's access to me. I have an unlisted phone number and then make sure those few who have it know that I don't like to be disturbed by phone calls. In case access by email is still letting too many people through the filter, I frequently change my email address. I tweet but don't respond to most personal messages on Twitter, and I have a Facebook page on which I regularly post—but only because of the controlled access it offers. You might think that I do this because I am so popular that people are beating down the door to gain access to me. You might even charitably assume that I am too busy doing other important things to allow these sorts of direct personal contacts. But this is rubbish. I simply want to indulge my preference to avoid interruptions and live my life as I want to live it rather than as it actually comes to me.

I tell myself that I am just a very private person (which is true), that I highly value solitude (which is also true), and that I want to protect my space so I can live my calling as a writer (also true). But these are rationalizations. As much as I love going with the flow of life, I also want to protect myself from awareness of the anxiety associated with living life in a truly open manner. My lust for control is strong, but in spite of knowing how that cuts me off from life, I still cling to it because it offers some degree of protection from the annoying background existential anxiety that comes from being human.

The anxiety is not the problem. The problem is our avoidance of it. Anxiety isn't a demon we need to exorcise. It's a messenger coming from our depths with a vitally important message: the human self is frail and vulnerable. Denying awareness of that fact does nothing to change our vulnerability; it only cut us off from our depths. True freedom does not come from control but from surrender. It comes from letting go of our illusions and engaging life with all its messiness, unpredictability, and risks. This requires courage and trust, but it is the only route to the fullness and wholeness of being human.

To understand the wholeness of being human, we first need to better understand the wholeness of being itself. As we begin to understand the foundational operating principle of the cosmos as the pull toward wholeness that ripples through it, we get a big-picture overview of the nature of human wholeness and see important contours of the journey we must take if we are to move toward it. Take a deep breath and fasten your seat belt before turning the page because the big picture is *really* big, and the ride we will be going on as we explore it is quite a ride!

2

Cosmic Interconnectedness

John Donne was right when he wrote, "No man is an island, entire of itself."[1] No one exists in isolation. We may have no close friends, and we may feel disconnected from our families, but everyone has a mother and a father, who themselves were part of families, which were part of communities, cultures, countries, and humankind all traveling together with the rest of us on this lifeboat called earth. Every one of us has a history of relationships that are an important part of who we are today.

Furthermore, as demographers like to point out, we are all also a part of a cohort of those who were born within a culture at a particular point in time, and these demographic groups do much more to define individuals than most of us realize.[2] For myself, I am near the leading edge of the baby boomers, the group of people in North America who were born between 1946 and 1964 and who, because of their massive numbers, have been a major force of cultural change as they pass through their life cycle. Demographic groups have a powerful influence not only on society but also on their individual members. Even those who view themselves as outliers to their culture and tradition are much more like their demographic cohort than they might think.[3]

Everything that exists forms a part of a larger whole and finds its ultimate place within that larger sphere. No one is an island unto him- or herself; even islands cluster to form archipelagos, which cluster with neighboring landmasses to form countries, which exist as parts of continents, which form a part of earth, which is one planet orbiting around a sun in a galaxy that is one of the 170 billion galaxies in the observable universe—a universe that has been continuously expanding since the Big Bang 14.6 billion years ago. And when we go in the opposite direction, we see the same thing: larger wholes enfolding smaller wholes right down to the subatomic level where molecules enfold atoms, which in turn enfold protons, neutrons, and electrons, which enfold quarks, and on it goes. Life is an infinite series of nesting Russian dolls—from infinitesimally small subatomic ones that no existing technology allows us to see to the most expansive ones that exist at the cosmic level and that are beyond our present ability to observe. Everything that is exists within this nesting of life.

Modern science confirms the fundamental insight of perennial wisdom that everything exists as little wholes within larger wholes. But the little wholes that form part of the larger whole do not operate independently. They are all interrelated in an artful, choreographed dance, which is the basic pattern of the universe that was first detected in biology but has since been identified in the other major natural and human sciences. It is the most basic pattern of life.

Nothing in the world is ultimately intelligible apart from its relationship to the larger wholes in which it exists, and humans are very much included within this pattern. Isn't it curious, therefore, how science tends to take things apart and examine parts in isolation of the whole in an attempt to understand the whole? We tend to do the same when we reflect on who we are or when we introduce ourselves to others.

Several years ago I had the privilege of serving as a delegate to the hearings and dialogue circles organized by the Truth and Reconciliation Commission of Canada around a shameful but important chapter in Canadian history. Over 157 years, more than 150,000 First Nations children between the ages of six and fifteen were forcibly removed from their families and communities all across Canada in order to eradicate any residue of their language, culture, or former aboriginal identity. One of the dialogue circles I was invited to attend involved a number of First Nations chiefs and elders on Vancouver Island, where I was living at the time. I knew I would be one of only two or three non-Aboriginals in attendance, but I didn't expect to be immediately asked to introduce myself to the group. Not being very familiar with their culture, I thought I should keep what I said as short as possible—speaking my name, saying a couple of things about who I was, mentioning how honored I was to be invited to meet with them, and then sitting down. As soon as I was finished, a man to my right in the circle stood up and began to speak. First he told us about his grandfather on his mother's side—why he was named as he was and several hilariously funny stories about his life. Then he drifted into stories about his grandmother and her family. Then he did the same for his grandparents on his father's side. This led to stories about his father and mother, his uncles and aunts, and then his siblings. Then we heard about his children and twelve grandchildren. This went on for about twenty minutes before he said that he felt his ancestors were with us in the room. Others nodded in agreement. He then sat down, and the person to the other side of him stood and began to do much the same. Her story went on for about the same length of time. She wept as she told stories about her ancestors and laughed with delight as she spoke of her children and grandchildren. Then she expressed her gratitude for the presence of the ancestors and sat down. The next person rose to his feet and did the same—and so it continued for two hours. Finally finishing this introductory part of the meeting, we broke for coffee, and the man to my right spoke to me. He said he was glad I was there, but with a twinkle in his eye, he asked if I didn't have any family.

Nothing or no one is intelligible apart from the larger wholes within which we as smaller wholes exist. John Donne was right; to exist is to exist within a thick web of interconnections. And yet how often we reflect the individualism of our culture by pretending that we stand alone and are the sum of our personal history.

This insight about the interconnectedness of all things has important implications for my task in this book. The human brain, for example, is not ultimately intelligible without considering the whole human person. And the human person is not ultimately intelligible apart from the family and community within which he or she exists. Furthermore, humans are not intelligible without reference to the transcendent horizon within which they exist and to which their deepest longings point. Things can be understood only from the perspective of the whole. Little wholes can be understood only in relation to the larger wholes within which they exist.

Psychology has, for the most part, studied humans apart from the larger context within which we belong. This has seriously limited the resulting understanding of persons. Sociology and anthropology complement psychology by introducing the element of culture that is missing in its overly individualistic focus. Philosophy and religion also help us to understand important dimensions of human being and becoming—dimensions that are crucial if we are to understand the ultimate meaning and purpose of being human. However, for the largest perspective, we need to turn to cosmology, for here we find the broadest available understanding of our place within the cosmos.

The Great Nest of Being

Cosmologists are the cartographers of existence. It is their job to develop big-picture maps that cover the totality of existence in a way that shows how the various data points on that map relate to one another. It is their maps that are, therefore, of the most help to us as we seek to understand the web of cosmic interconnections within which humans exist.

One of the best-known maps of everything that exists comes to us from the wisdom tradition, which will be a continuing reference point throughout this book. It is usually called the Great Chain of Being.[4] The wonderful thing about this map is that it is as relevant to the unfolding of the human self as it is to the unfolding of the cosmos. It is a map that spans the range from dust to divinity and shows the integral and dynamic relationship that exists among everything that is.

Traditionally, the Great Chain of Being is organized around five levels of existence (matter, life, mind, soul, and spirit) that are usually presented as links in a chain. Somewhat more helpfully, these five levels of existence are sometimes presented as a series of concentric circles with matter being at the core and spirit forming the outermost ring. But since reality is not a two-dimensional flatland, perhaps we can improve the image even further by adding a third dimension. Now imagine those five levels extending upward into an ever-opening, three-dimensional cone. Picture it as a slinky cone—a continuous coil that is made up of ever-widening rings. Matter is now at the bottom of the narrow end of this cone, followed by life, mind, soul, and spirit as it opens in ever-widening rings to hold everything that exists. Viewed in this way, the great chain becomes the great nest in which everything that exists finds its home and its place.

The most basic level of existence is matter. Matter is the darkest form of existence because it is the densest of all the levels of being. Everything else that exists emerged out of matter, getting closer and closer to spirit and, consequently, less and less dense.[5]

But notice something important about movement up through higher levels of existence. Each higher level emerges out of the level beneath it, integrating the lower level and only then transcending it. Life involves the enlivening of matter and therefore includes

The Spiral Dynamics of Awakening

Spirit

Soul

Mind

Life

Matter

matter. In the same way, mind includes both life and matter, although it is not reducible to either. It transcends both and can never be accounted for strictly in terms of the lower levels that it subsumes. Mind is more than brain. It has its own emergent properties that transcend both matter and life. Consciousness, thought, memory, will, imagination, and emotion are all mental processes that are grounded in the physical brain, but they also transcend the brain. In the same way, soul and spirit also transcend but include everything below them.

The Great Nest of Being tells us that higher levels of existence emerge from lower levels but are not reducible to them. Matter includes only itself, but each of the higher levels includes all lower levels while at the same time transcending them.

Each level of existence enfolds all lower levels. Plotinus, a major third-century CE contributor to the development of the perennial wisdom tradition, describes the nesting as "development that is envelopment."[6] Forward movement (development) does not involve moving beyond a lower level but an integration within the self (envelopment) and then a carrying forth into new expressions. Unfolding does not mean abandoning lower levels of existence. It means no longer being limited to them. But let's go back to the image of the nesting Russian dolls. While each level of existence is whole in and of itself, at the same time each is a part of a larger whole that contains but transcends the smaller wholes of lower levels.

Being and Becoming

One important implication of this map of existence is that it helps us to understand the context of human being and the direction of human becoming. Humans carry in their being all five levels of existence: matter, life, mind, soul, and spirit. As described by the Judeo-Christian creation story, humans are made of dust that is enlivened by divine breath.[7] To be human, therefore, is to be a creature of the material world but to carry within the self a vitality that comes from the spiritual world. Whatever spirituality is, it should not be something that pulls us away from the material world. To be human is to have a fundamental attachment to the earth that should never be relinquished as we cultivate higher levels of being. Transcending a level of being paradoxically involves deepening our engagement with it as we weave that strand of our being ever more securely into the fabric of our existence.

In the same way, mind builds on everything below it as it includes both life and matter. The human mind, as we discovered in chapter 1, contains much more than reason. It also includes such subtle faculties as intuition, imagination, symbol formation and manipulation, extrasensory perception, body wisdom, and attending to our deep emotions, moods, and shifting ego states.

The mind is seriously constrained when it operates only on the logical and linear processes of reason. But when it is firing on all the cylinders at its disposal, it is a critically important dimension of human being.

Forgetting the ancient wisdom of the perennial tradition, the West generally views the mind as the capstone of human existence. We enshrine its cultivation, viewing the mind as that which most distinctively makes us human, but the consequences of this for those who have lower levels of intellectual development or capacity are tragic. By implication, they are less than fully human. And this is precisely how they are generally treated. But persons who are developmentally delayed or suffering from forms of brain damage that involve cognitive impairment are no more subhuman than those who are short, have impaired hearing, or were born with a bad heart.

As important as the mind is, it is not the essence of human being. All is not lost when mental powers begin to decline. As both mind and body begin to wane from their peaks of prowess in our twenties and thirties, we are given a natural opportunity to turn inward and attend to the cultivation of the more hidden and much more ignored dimensions of soul and spirit.

Soul is the womb of experience. James Hillman describes it as the middle ground between matter and spirit.[8] It exists in the reflective space between events and experience, mind and body, being and doing. It is a way of seeing and living with depth. Soul generates meaning by connecting spirit to experience. Standing in this middle ground, it plays a vital role in holding us together and in grounding us in the world, in the body, in the thick of things—especially in the dark, painful, messy, and confusing parts of life. The soul's connection to the dark and painful places explains why, at times, we want to escape it. At the same time, it also makes clear why a spiritual flight from this place can lead only to disaster as life is no longer tethered to material realities.

The call of soul is a call to belonging, descent, and grounding. Soul penetrates deep within particularities of our lives. It invites us to learn what the lessons of triumph and achievement can never teach us. Only suffering and struggle—experiences we would never choose—will grow a soul big enough to hold our life. This happens when we ground ourselves in the blood, sweat, and tears of ordinary life. Rather than rising above these things, soul calls us to find life and meaning in the midst of them.

While the call of soul is to deeply engage the mundane details of daily existence, the call of spirit is to pursue cosmic heights and the farthest reaches of our being. The call of spirit is up and out, beyond the self, to places of self-transcendence and spaciousness. Spirit calls us on a journey to follow our longings as we are drawn toward self-transcendent soaring. Spirit is expansive, always questing, driven by deep longings. Spirit calls us to encounter that which is beyond the individual self. It calls us to settle for nothing less than our true home. As we move toward this, we transcend the particulars of our own small, often cramped lives and find our meaning, place, and calling in a larger, much vaster place than the small ego-self could ever imagine.

Spirit is the fire in our belly. Without it we would live as machines, not as humans. To lose our spirit is to be on a deathwatch, since spirit is life. It is the vitalizing spark that exists in our depths. It gives purpose and direction to life. It is the dynamic and enriching force that enables us to live life to the full. Like fire and wind, spirit ignites, moves, and animates. Spirit is our most subtle form of energy. It is our connection to our source and our destiny. It is our divine DNA. Without spirit, we have no true life, since it is ultimately both our source and destiny.

Full unfolding of human personhood involves movement from matter to life, to mind, to soul, and finally and fully to spirit. But it is important to remember that movement to higher levels never leaves behind lower levels. Development is based on envelopment—picture the Russian dolls! Becoming does not mean abandoning lower levels of existence but no longer being limited to them. Human becoming always means increasing wholeness.

Spirit is the goal of the entire sequence of this journey toward integral wholeness. All of life is flowing in its direction, that is, toward greater consciousness and greater complexity, but at the same time greater unity and integral wholeness. All life emerges from God and is moving back into God.[9]

What this means is that the gentle pull to be become more than you are—more whole, more free, more fully and deeply human—is the wooing of spirit drawing you back into the ground of your being. You might have been treating your growth as a self-improvement project, but in reality, it has been consent to this flow of life drawing all things toward spirit.

A friend recently told me how he had been surprised to notice a significant softening of attachment to his appearance. The surprise lay in the fact that this wasn't something he had been trying to change. He told me that he noticed that instead of always thinking about his body and how he looked, his thoughts and passions were now much more focused on the care of the earth. Since I had last seen him, he had become involved with a nature conservancy foundation and this had, he said, helped him "get over himself." Far from simply being the byproduct of a new pastime, the inner shifts he was experiencing were the result of his deeper movement into the flow of spirit drawing him and everything that exists back toward the Ground of Being. This did not involve a rejection of his body—something that would have alarmed me if this had been what he had reported—but rather the realization that he was more than his material self.

Everything that exists participates in this flow. But only humans need to offer their consent in order to participate in it. Only humans seem capable of withholding their cooperation and staunching (or at least restricting) the flow of becoming. This is why humans hold such an important role in the future of evolution.

Evolutionary Whole-Making

Evolution is the movement toward increasing wholeness. It is the process of the complexification of energy that results in a rise of consciousness, which eventually expresses itself in awareness. It is the growing of smaller wholes into larger wholes. It is a cosmic journey of becoming. From a Christian point of view, all of this happens under the dynamic impulse of God's creative power and love, because God is at the heart of the evolutionary process, empowering it from within.[10]

The foundational force operating within evolution that gives rise to integral wholes cannot be explained by science. Science can only describe its operation. Physicist Paul Davies describes it as the self-organizing nature of the universe.[11] Without contradicting the second law of thermodynamics (which describes the nature of entropy in closed systems), Davies and many others affirm that the universe is an open system that can increase in order and complexity through concentrations of energy that allow things to cross thresholds. When these thresholds are crossed, part-wholes become more whole as they participate in the wholeness of the larger wholes of their ultimate belonging.

We see this tendency to whole-making in cosmic history when, sometime after the initial Big Bang explosion that birthed the universe, particles began to cool and move toward one another, clustering together to form larger wholes. This foundational pattern seems to be in place wherever we look in the universe since then. What we see is a weaving of partial wholes into larger ones. This, and the associated growth of consciousness, is what Teilhard de Chardin describes as the goal of evolution. Far from random, the path of evolution is a persistent pull toward increasing wholeness, complexity, and consciousness. The dynamic character of being implies the tendency of every-thing to transcend itself and express itself in ever-evolving and new ways.

It appears that the cosmos is held together by the energy of consciousness and—as we shall see later—love. As life becomes more
complex and conscious, it becomes more whole. As it becomes
more whole, it becomes more conscious and more complex, and
that complexity is held together by love.

This also describes the overall framework of human becoming.
Higher levels of consciousness and identity are considered higher
precisely because they involve larger wholes. The journey toward
increasing wholeness is quite different from the journey toward
increasing perfection. Wholeness isn't the elimination of inconsistencies and the shadow aspects of personality but an integration of
them. As more and more previously lost and rejected parts of self
are embraced and woven together with the rest of personhood, the
result is a larger whole. Wholeness doesn't involve getting our act
together but becoming a truer and more integral self. It recognizes
the reality of the larger self that we truly are as we integrate parts
that were previously considered to be non-self.

Movement to increasing wholeness always involves an expansion of identity and consciousness.[12] If the expansion of identity takes the form of the integration of previously alienated and
rejected parts of self, the expansion of consciousness takes the
form of recognizing the illusory nature of the separate self and
conscious participation in the larger whole that now forms the core
of our identity. Taken together, these transformations of identity
and consciousness represent human evolution at the level of the
individual.[13]

Seeing through the Optical Illusion

There is, of course, a truth that lies at the core of what I call the
"optical illusion" of the separate self. We are and always will be
distinguishable from any other person within the larger groups
in which we exist. Larger wholes do not involve a fusion of the

part-wholes that exist within them. Smaller wholes have integrity and uniqueness that make them worthy to be described as wholes in themselves. That is not the illusion of which I speak. Smaller wholes are simply part of larger wholes. Finding our place within those larger wholes does not mean becoming lost within some amorphous blob. We remain unique but not separate. However, we become more whole whenever we find our place within larger wholes.

Musical notes do not lose their essential nature when they form a part of a symphony. But one note does not a symphony make, even though without the notes there is no symphony. Wholes are much more than the sum of their parts, and a symphony can have a grandeur and power that a single note can never have. Larger wholes need the cooperation and contribution of the smaller part-wholes. They belong together.

The great optical illusion relates to the sense of separateness that we normally experience when we think of ourselves versus others or the world. This is a product of the binary operating system that I will describe in a later chapter as the default mode of consciousness. In this mode of consciousness, everything gets divided and classified as a way of ordering the vast, buzzing array of reality. Binary classifications like good versus bad, attractive versus unattractive, or "like me" versus "not like me" get made in an astoundingly efficient manner. We are usually unaware of making a judgment; it simply seems that we are recognizing an obvious truth. However, any classification involves distortion as part of its simplification, and nowhere is this truer than in binary classifications.

While all binary classifications have important psychological and spiritual consequences, the one that stands out as having the greatest impact on consciousness is the judgment about what *is* me versus what *is not* me. Chances are excellent that you will be surprised to hear this. It seems obvious that I am not you, and you are not me. How could we ever question this ostensible fact?

As an infant, one is taught to identify with *my* nose and *my* toes, and by three years old one usually has a sense of *my* body being separate from that of anyone else. One also has a sense that *my* skin contains the separate self that by then one has come to think of as "me."

However, what is obvious at one level of consciousness is quite different from what is obvious at another. Mystics report knowing, not simply believing, something that sounds absurd from the perspective of the lower levels of consciousness most of the rest of us occupy. They speak of experiencing a pervasive sense of oneness with everything that is. This does not mean that they think they are a tree, a bird, some other person, or God. It means that they experience a profound solidarity and at-oneness with everything and everyone. It means that they sense the fundamental way in which they and we are deeply interconnected with everything else that exists, woven together at the very deepest levels of self. This is why they speak of the optical illusion of the separate self. They know that the self exists within a thick web of interconnectedness and is far from being as separate as it seems. What seems obvious is not always true!

Those who live with a sense of the enfolding and holding that comes from being part of larger wholes generally learn to be careful about whom they share this with. I think of a woman who was a natural mystic. She grew up with a deep sense of solidarity and communion with the trees, birds, and flowers that filled the backyard of her home. One day soon after she started school she made a terrible mistake. She told a girlfriend about her sense of closeness to the natural world. This friend laughed at her and told the other girls in their circle of friendship that she talked to trees. Speaking to me about these things many years later, she said that she had always felt God so profoundly that it was impossible to distinguish between what was God in her and what was her in God. She wondered if this made her crazy and came to me for a professional judgment. But she wasn't crazy; she was just unusually aware. She sensed things that others didn't sense and knew things that others couldn't comprehend.

It is important to distinguish this sort of mystical knowing from mere belief. It involves knowing, not simply thinking. It is as different from thinking as knowing the experience of love is from mere talk about love.

If you are attentive, you may notice times when you have had momentary glimpses of these possibilities. Perhaps it was a moment when you felt lost in something larger than yourself, or perhaps it felt more like you suddenly found your true self when you became aware of being a part of a larger whole. Possibly it was a moment that involved a temporary change in your sense of your self, and the self you discovered was larger and more inclusive. It may have been the solidarity you experienced with an athletic team and other fans of your team—particularly in the moment in which one of your teammates scored the winning goal, run, or point. Or it may have happened at a political rally, national celebration, or powerful religious event. In that moment your consciousness was expanded and your sense of identity enlarged. You knew that you are not alone. You knew that you are part of a larger whole, and that knowledge filled you with an inner buoyancy and sense of expansiveness.

These moments of altered consciousness are easily dismissed. But they involve a peek into a dimension of reality that can be known much more fully and continuously through a more permanent movement into a higher level of consciousness—a possibility we will explore later in this book.

The separate self is an illusion. The self is infinitely larger than what we experience as "me" because we are part of a larger whole—a whole that is itself but a part of an even larger whole. And on and on it goes. Our deepest human problems do not result from isolation but from a lack of awareness of the web of interconnections within which we are held. These interconnections can be known, not merely thought or believed. And doing so makes all the difference in the world!

Cosmic Estrangement

There may be no more painful ache of the soul than the sense of
estrangement. I have a friend who has lived for twenty years of
total estrangement from and rejection by her family—her children, her siblings, her aunts and uncles, her nieces and nephews.
All conspired to stand against her in judgment when she left her
husband, and all have continued to stand in solidarity in this act
of banishment. Her pain is immense and constant, as acute now
as it was twenty years ago. It shows no signs of lessening. There
is nothing she longs for more than to have her existence positively
acknowledged by even one member of her family.

But I have also worked with people whose sense of estrangement
is even deeper. They feel alone and hopelessly adrift in the cosmos.
Although they have friends, colleagues, and acquaintances, they
feel alienated from existence itself. Their sense of not belonging to
anyone or anywhere results in a deep uncertainty about their very
existence. I recall one man telling me that he lived with the deep
and terrifying sense that he was but a character in someone else's
dream. This man was not crazy. He was a very high-functioning
and successful architect. But he lived with a deep existential anxiety
that resulted in his feeling that he was never far from the edge of
an inner abyss of nonbeing. Staying well back from the edge of
this inner void consumed a great deal of energy and served as a
major block to the trust and surrender that was essential for his
further becoming. It also blocked his creativity. Although he was
very successful at what he did, he had always wanted to be an
artist but felt he couldn't risk letting go to a high enough degree
for that level of creative expression.

Over the years, I have encountered this sort of anxiety in varying
degrees in patients I have treated, which leads me to suspect that
psychologists have failed to give sufficient weight to the human
need to belong. Neither have we understood the magnitude of
the fault line that is opened up in the soul when a person has no

sense of belonging. To be cut off from the larger whole may be the core of human dysfunction. It may just be the taproot of all human dis-ease.

If this is true, knowing that the Great Nest of Being holds us is crucially important. All the great spiritual traditions proclaim this truth. All teach that we belong. All sketch similar contours of the framework within which we belong. And all point to spirit as the ultimate place of our belonging.

But how can we ever know this, rather than merely believe it, if the spiritual realm is as separate from the material as is often presented? There seems to be no hope for humanity if spirituality requires that we abandon this thick world of highly compressed energy to escape to the more subtle energy of a separate world of spirit. The only hope is if spirit is already here—among, between, and within us. If this is true, then the place where we can best come to know the web of interconnectedness within which we are held is right here in the midst of life with all its complications, contingencies, and complexity. This is the truth that is taught by the perennial wisdom tradition and by all major religions.[14]

Cosmic Reconnection

The route back to our place within the Great Nest of Belonging usually involves both descent and ascent. But whether we are moving up or down within the Great Nest of Being, we are given the opportunity to weave together the elements of existence that are most lacking in us.

The path of descent involves grounding ourselves in materiality—not materialism (which is altogether a different thing) but in the material realities of our existence. A great first step toward this is to befriend your body. Pay attention to it. Instead of trying to ignore it, listen to what it is telling you. As you do, you will learn to strengthen your relationship to matter. Be a good host to your material self. Don't ignore it, and don't treat it as the enemy. Welcome your body to your family-of-self and treat it with the gracious attentiveness and respect that good hospitality always involves.

You can also connect to materiality by strengthening your relationship with the natural world. From wherever you are right now, let your roots sink down into the earth beneath you, no matter how far below you that may be. Draw your vitality from that earth, and learn to cherish it. Treat it with the same hospitality with which I am suggesting that you treat your body, cherishing it as you would your own self. Begin to notice it as part of the ground of your being.

An honoring embrace of materiality is the single most important missing ingredient in most contemporary spiritualties—Christianity certainly included. Until the body and the earth are embraced, any spiritual journey will be seriously truncated. Both the body and the earth are sacred places because spirit is already present in them, but you will discover the spirit in materiality only as you make space for soulful engagement with material realities.

We need to *know* that we belong, not merely *believe* that we belong. And we can come to know this only through deep and continuing engagement with material realities, soulful reflection on and holding of the questions and tensions that arise in doing so, and careful attention to the stirrings in our spirits that alert us to the subtle shifts in energy that reflect the presence of spirit.

Though we tend to rush the process of making our home in our bodies, we will never be at home anywhere else until we do so. Many of us know the limitations of living in our heads and strive to live in our souls or spirits instead. But authentic habitation of our souls or spirits can arise only out of deep, meaningful, and ongoing engagement with our bodies. Paradoxically, the only way to ascend to spirit is to first descend into matter. But if this descent is to ultimately lead to further ascent, we must bring our spirit, soul, and mind with us, for only then can we ever hope to find meaning in materiality.

3

Meaning-Making

Humans are meaning-seeking creatures. The question of "why" is one that springs to our lips—or at least to our minds—whenever things happen to us that are distinctively unwelcome. Seldom do we ask "why" if we win the lottery, find a great love, or get a promotion at work. But when we experience a major financial reversal, undergo the death of a loved one, or are diagnosed with cancer, the "why" question often preoccupies us. It is interesting to note that we do not seem to be surprised when bad things happen to others. But when they happen to us or those we love, we are deeply distressed because it challenges our unspoken but unrealistic expectations about how life is supposed to operate. In other words, it challenges our system of meaning. Asking why things are happening to us will seldom lead to an explanation of the unwelcome events. However, it does give us a chance to update our framework of meaning and, hopefully, allow it to better support us in living the reality that actually is our life.

Asking "why" may well be a distinctively human trait. It emerges in the space between the events of our life and our most essential self—the space I call soul. This is the place within us that invites us to avoid defaulting to the automatic response mode that is part of our vestigial, instinctual heritage. It invites us to engage the experience with reflection, which allows us to act, not simply react. Soulful reflection is indispensable to the growth of our inner self and the enhancement of its freedom, and meaning-making forms an important part of both of these things.

We never achieve meaning in a final form. New experiences—particularly if they involve loss or suffering—always demand that we revisit our system of meaning as we try to fit new experience within our evolving life story. Neither can we inherit meaning from others—whether it be friends, family, or religious tradition. Any meaning that has a chance of being meaningful must be created, not simply received. It must arise as a personal response to our life. A philosophical or religious statement of the meaning of life in general is useless until it is refined and personalized by reflecting on our experience. Therefore, systems of meaning are always dynamic, always evolving. To turn them into something rigid and fixed is to render them useless; that which is no longer evolving is either devolving or dead.

Beings, Not Billiard Balls

One of the most important ways in which human beings differ from inanimate forms of life is that humans are not bound by the same mechanical laws of cause and effect. Strike a billiard ball with a certain amount of force and spin from a specified angle on a billiard table, and there is no mystery as to exactly where or how fast it will go. But strike a human and the result will be much less predictable—and perhaps quite surprising!

I have already expressed my conviction that humans do not need to be victims of their history. The human capacity for meaning-making

lies at the center of this remarkable alchemical ability to transmute
bad into good and thereby transcend experiences.

The teenage Etty Hillesum—who was Jewish by birth but
never subsequently identified with any specific religious tradition—found compassion and inner peace in the midst of the Nazi
roundup of Jews in Amsterdam. Early in her diary we encounter a
young woman who is moody and self-absorbed—just about what
one might expect, considering her age and life circumstances.[1]
However, as the horror of the concentration camps closes in on
her, she finds God in the midst of circumstances that we might
have expected would have made her angry, fearful, or full of despair. Instead, she becomes freer than she had ever been in her
short life—altruistic, serene, and full of wonder as she discovers
beauty everywhere and meaning in the most horrific circumstances
imaginable. She is never a victim. Instead, she discovers the mystery of meaning-making as the route to inner freedom, and the
meaning she makes of her life leads to a deeper and fuller life in
the midst of circumstances no one would ever willingly choose.

Nelson Mandela also comes to mind when I think of people
who have risen dramatically above their life history and circumstances. After twenty-seven years of imprisonment (much of it in
solitary confinement) for his opposition to apartheid, he made a
place of special honor for his former jailer at his inauguration as
the president of South Africa. Prison was not simply a place of
confinement and punishment; it was his alchemical laboratory. It
was where an angry young freedom fighter was transformed into
a gentle, compassionate, and wise statesman who became the
nation's voice of reconciliation. Base materials were transformed
into gold as he came to understand the depths of his solidarity
with all humans—including his captors. The meaning that he
found in his suffering and solitude allowed him to recognize that
freedom is indivisible. It allowed him to recognize that as long as
anyone remains in chains, everyone remains in chains.[2] This was
how he knew that those who imprisoned him were in the same

bondage and that *his* freedom was as dependent on their release from hatred as *their* freedom was on his ability to forgive them. Long before his circumstances changed and he was released from prison, he found meaning that released him from his imprisonment within his small, angry ego-self and began to live out of the much more expansive places of his spirit.

The only meaning that ever stands a chance of having this sort of transformational potential is one that is large enough to provide a context for dealing with suffering and makes life itself— not merely what one can get out of life—the ultimate ground of personal meaning.

The Gifts of Suffering

Please do not misunderstand me. By speaking of gifts that can potentially be found in suffering, I am not trying to spin suffering into a good thing. Anyone who does so has never really suffered.

However, suffering can play a tremendously important role not just in meaning-making but also in preparing us for the transformational possibilities associated with the farther reaches of human becoming. Suffering tests whatever provisional meanings of life we have developed and invites us to deepen them. Ultimately, we need a meaning that will be strong enough to make suffering sufferable. This is the crucial test of any personal framework of meaning. But for meaning to be useful, it has to help us live life as it actually is, not as we wish it might be. In order to do that, it has to help us cope with suffering, loss, and death.

Few of us do much work on refining our ever-evolving personal framework of meaning when life appears to be going well. When life is good, its purpose seems self-evident—to enjoy life. But the superficiality of this meaning system only becomes evident when life is not so good. Only then do we feel the need for a framework to make sense of life and help us cope with it.

One of the worst things a psychotherapist can do is relieve people of their suffering before they have helped them discover its meaning. Suffering is not in itself a good thing, but it does come with potential gifts that are unwrapped only when we are prepared to resist the instinctive response of trying to eliminate the suffering. While there are many ways to lessen suffering—be they chemical, psychological, or spiritual—there is only one way to learn from it.

Paradoxically, the only way in which we can discover the gifts that suffering brings to us is to open ourselves to it. We must meet it at the door of the self and welcome it with hospitality. I realize that this is counterintuitive. Our default response is to resist suffering, but resistance serves only to close down our inner soul-space. To do so is to close down our only hope of thriving within suffering rather than simply coping with it. If we are to make suffering bearable we must first embrace it, not fight it.

The thirteenth-century Sufi mystic Rumi understood this well and expresses the point powerfully in his poem *The Guest House*.

> This being human is a guest house.
> Every morning a new arrival.
> A joy, a depression, a meanness,
> some momentary awareness comes
> as an unexpected visitor.
>
> Welcome and entertain them all!
> Even if they are a crowd of sorrows,
> who violently sweep your house
> empty of its furniture,
> still, treat each guest honourably . . .
> because each has been sent
> as a guide from beyond.[3]

Showing hospitality to suffering is not the same as pretending to be happy that you are suffering. It isn't a posture of pretense. It is a posture of welcoming openness.

Our default response to something unpleasant is usually to tense our muscles and prepare to fight or resist it. But it is that inner posture of bracing ourselves for battle that cuts us off from life much more than the actual suffering. It is like holding our breath—eventually, it will kill us!

Showing hospitality to suffering starts with releasing that inner constriction. Letting it go makes space for you to meet and show hospitality to the uninvited guest that has suddenly appeared in your home. Rather than trying to drive suffering out, get to know it. Listen to it—to the questions it asks of you, not the questions you want to ask of it. Be gentle with it, and it will reveal its secrets to you. Allow it to just be what it is, as it is. As you do, you will begin to discover the gifts it brings to you.

Don't confuse these gifts with lessons you are supposed to learn from the suffering. That is just a mind game, a kind of quid pro quo by which you hope that if you offer some form of penance, the suffering will go away. Hospitality can't be a guise for an attempt to get rid of the uninvited guest. It must be a genuine offer of willingness to welcome the guest and patiently wait to see what gifts you might receive from the encounter—how it might deepen your framework of meaning for life.

Accepting suffering is a spiritual response of great potential power. It allows us to release anger and resentment. It allows our meaning system to support us in the face of something beyond the limits of our power of control. The acceptance of suffering invites us to engage the suffering with openness, thus grounding our meaning *in* life, not merely some theoretical meaning *of* life.

Finding Meaning, Living Meaningfully

What we ultimately need to make suffering sufferable is not a philosophical or theological meaning of suffering but eyes to see the meaningfulness of living. What we need is not to figure out the meaning of life but to discover a meaningful way of *living* life. For this to happen, we must allow the meaning to emerge from life itself, not what we can get out of it. This is the essence of spirituality, which is, at its core, a way of living life in relation to a self-transcendent framework of meaning and purpose.

Until life itself is recognized as the greatest gift we could ever receive, our meaning in life will be based on trying to force our lives into some form that pleases us and gives us the things we count to be meaningful—things like happiness, fulfillment, love, and esteem. When we are happy and feel at least to some extent fulfilled, we regard life as meaningful. But this confuses a meaningful life with a happy one.

Basing the meaningfulness of life on our happiness will never be strong enough to withstand the inevitable losses, suffering, and diminishment that always come with human existence. The seasons of life include both waxing and waning, success and failure, great joy and great sadness. Happiness and fulfillment will never be strong enough to hold us when we receive a terminal diagnosis and suddenly face a greatly shortened life expectancy. How will you live in those last six months if everything points to the probability that you will die within them? And what will it take to make your life during those months meaningful?

I wrote this last paragraph in the shadow of the immanent death of my only sibling, my younger brother. He lived well, and based on what I saw from a distance (he was living in Thailand while I was in Canada), he seemed to be preparing to die well. But I have just now returned from a final good-bye visit with him, and I know much more about the way in which meaning can make suffering sufferable. He died while I was flying home, but we had several days of good conversation about how he was facing his death. I struggle to write of these conversations, and yet I feel I cannot discuss meaningful living and dying with authenticity unless I do so.

Colin was diagnosed with liver cancer just after moving to Bangkok and died ten months later.[4] He moved there to pastor an expat church, something he had been doing for thirty years in nine different countries. His life had been one of service. When I arrived for this final goodbye, he had just been moved from a multi-bed room in a hospital to a private room in a hospice because he was distressed to be unable to help the people who were suffering and dying around him. Helping people in times of distress had been his life and calling, and the meaning he had found in earlier stages of life served him extremely well in his last days. Until a week before he died, he continued to post weekly blogs about his journey through the last stage of his life. I had been reading these in Canada and was a bit concerned that the peace he said he was feeling about dying might be built on denial. When I saw him, I knew that was not the case.

I asked him about his experience of dying. He told me that dying was easy but that letting go of those he loved was hard. His family was central to what made living meaningful. He told me that he knew that he would remain a vital and enduring part of each of us, and this gave him peace as he was preparing for his last breath. When I asked about how he had been living these recent days when he knew that his death was immanent, he spoke much of the enormous satisfaction he experienced from knowing that he had lived his calling. He told me that he had received hundreds of email and Facebook messages from around the world. Many people told him that he had taught them more in the last six months of his journey through this last stage of life than he had in the whole time they had known him. I told him I understood what they were saying because this was my experience as well.

Systems of meaning that are strong enough to weave even death within the fabric of a meaningful life will always have a reference point beyond our own happiness. Fortunately, we do not have to wait until death knocks at our door to develop a truly meaningful way of living our life. Every loss can be a preparation for death if it is engaged with soulful reflection and updates our purpose for living.

I have long used weddings, funerals, and other stage-of-life rituals in this way. I now go to more funerals than weddings, but I make a point of using each as an opportunity to reflect on my own life and its meaning. I also make a point of talking with people older than I, particularly those who are ill or suffering, about what makes their life meaningful and how this helps them deal with their suffering. Many speak of their family. Some speak of their faith. Some continue to try to find meaning in their accomplishments and reputation. These are the ones I feel most sad for as I watch the inadequacy of that system of meaning become more and more apparent.

When life itself is received as the greatest gift we could ever receive, we move away from trying to force it into a shape that will make us happy and toward accepting it as it is. This shift from willfulness to willingness opens us to the possibility of a life based on consent rather than opposition.

Consenting to the Flow of Life

Life will be discovered to be meaningful only when we dare to receive it as it actually comes to us. I don't pretend that this is easy, particularly when our present realities are things that we would not naturally welcome. But this shift from willfully trying to force life into a shape that pleases us to a willing acceptance of life in its full reality is vitally important if we are to find the meaning that already exists in our lives.

A meaningful life emerges from living with a full-hearted "yes" of consent to life. What we are consenting to is not simply life as it is in the moment but life as it will continue to come to us. Life is much more like a river than a lake; it is dynamic and ever changing. Since we can't ultimately change or control it, withholding consent does not change anything but us. It cuts us off from life. In contrast, offering our consent aligns us with life and prepares us to go with its flow rather than swim against its current.

Unfortunately, we are defined as much by those things to which we say "no" as we are by those things to which we say "yes." Dis-identification and rejection do not remove from our being the things we make central to our identity by the embrace of a "no." We must, therefore, be as discerning in saying "no" as we are in saying "yes."

Richard Rohr points out that the ego strengthens itself by constriction, by being against things.[5] This is the way it defends against the loss it fears might come from opening and is also why "no" always comes easier than "yes." In contrast, the soul lives by expansion, not constriction. The soul thrives on the openness of a "yes," which is so terrifying to the ego. With all the vulnerability that is always part of openness, the soul leads us forward with a "yes" of affirmation and consent to life.

Dag Hammarskjöld, the second secretary general of the United Nations, understood the importance of offering this sort of affirmation and consent. In his book *Markings*, he speaks of his experience of offering a life-affirming "yes": "I don't know Who—or what—put the question. I don't know when it was put. I don't even remember answering it. But at some moment I did answer Yes to Someone—or Something—and from that hour I was certain that existence is meaningful and that, therefore, my life, in self-surrender, had a goal."[6]

"Yes" expresses openness to life. However, it is an openness that involves risk because it invites abandon and vulnerability. Only in this naked vulnerability can life itself be found to be meaningful.

Meaningful ways of living are never found in the safety of an armchair or ivory tower. They are found in the risky, vulnerable places of real life. They are found in living, not in books, lectures, or sermons. Ideas presented in books may come to form a place in a meaningful life, but if they are to help make suffering sufferable and life meaningful they will always be rooted in an openness to and affirmation of life as it is.

Pushing the River

But perhaps this sounds like too passive a way to live life. Maybe it feels like resignation instead of a truly vital engagement.

I recently met a rather remarkable woman, who happened to be sitting beside me on a long flight. As we began to talk, I soon discovered that she was eighty-nine years old, was about to get her airplane pilot's license, rode a Harley Davidson motorcycle, remained an active scuba diver, and was just returning from a hang-gliding holiday in the Rocky Mountains. She told me that her life philosophy was summed up by *carpe diem*—"seize the moment." She said that she intended to leave life as she lived it, running full throttle on the highest-octane gas she could pump into her engine—this including as many recreational drugs and as much alcohol and sex as she could safely consume or participate in. She was definitely not what I would have expected if you told me that my seatmate was going to be an eighty-nine-year-old woman, but she was one of the most interesting people I had met in quite a while!

This woman presents us with another perspective on what openness to life might involve. I have a great deal of admiration for her vitality and passionate embrace of life. However, there is quite a difference between her strategy for making life meaning-ful and the posture of openness to life's inherent meaning that I am describing. I understand why she hoped to leave life as she lived it. She said she couldn't think of anything better than dying in the midst of one of her moments of full-throttle engagement with life. I suspect that she would find an engagement with her decline intolerably distressing. Her lifestyle and worldview had not included making space in her soul to hold tension or grow her system of meaning. Dying was not going to be a stage of life but simply the end of life—the one thing she couldn't escape by her frantic pursuit of stimulation.

Openness to life isn't the same thing as an addiction to excite-ment. By participating in the flow of life we come to know the meaning and gift of life as it is. Pushing the river to increase the flow—or pushing against the flow to create our own counterflow—is currently a culturally popular way of engaging life. Ultimately, however, it is driven by egoic willfulness and lacks the vulnerability and true openness to life that is involved in a posture of willing consent and affirmation of reality as it is.

Purposeful Living

Meaning and purpose are closely related when it comes to life. Talk of purpose reminds us of the basic point I have been making in this chapter, namely, that the meaning that is created by how we live is what really counts when it comes to making suffering sufferable and life meaningful. But humans tend to live as if the purpose of life is self-evident. Unfortunately, the purpose that is self-evident is too small and narcissistic to be useful in holding us through waxing and waning, success and failure, great joy and great sadness. It is a purpose that lacks the necessary self-transcendence to truly integrate life and hold us within the Great Nest of Being that I discussed in chapter 2.

Ultimately, we humans need to look beyond the limited horizon of our own selves to discern the bigger purpose that connects us to the larger wholes within which we exist. In connecting us to those wholes, it will provide us with the framework that will guide us toward greater wholeness in ourselves.

Fritz Künkel has developed a whole psychology around finding our place, meaning, and purpose in relation to the larger wholes that transcend and enfold us.[7] As we become conscious of our relationship to these wholes and find our place within them, we feel like a tool seized by a strong hand. We also discover the purpose we are called to serve. Much larger than our job or role within our family or community, this is our vocation in the world.

The language of calling and vocation sounds somewhat strange to our modern ears. It comes to us from the Judeo-Christian tradition but has its roots in perennial wisdom. Rather than discussing it as an abstract concept, let me return to the story of Nelson Mandela to look more carefully at how he found his calling in the service of the larger whole.

Rolihlahla Mandela was born July 18, 1918, in Umtata, South Africa. His father, Henry Mandela, was chief of the Xhosa-speaking Tembu tribe. As a child, Rolihlahla—who was later given the English name of Nelson by his teacher on his first day at school—was deeply immersed in the traditions and worldview of this tribe. One part of this immersion that he was later to identify as foundational to his identity was the pan-African spiritual philosophy of Ubuntu. Reduced to its simplest form, Ubuntu is often expressed in the following terms: "I am because we are; we are because I am."

I first encountered Ubuntu when I was invited to give a series of lectures in South Africa on forgiveness and reconciliation several months after Nelson Mandela was elected president in South Africa's first all-race elections. The government had just established the framework for its Truth and Reconciliation hearings, and the whole nation was talking about the relationship between truth-telling, forgiveness, reconciliation, and national healing. It was an immense privilege to be present and able to participate in these discussions.

As part of that process, I heard the stories of a number of victims of trauma and torture and the abuse they endured under the apartheid regime. I had been working with victims of trauma and torture in North America for quite some time and so was not as shocked by the reports of what happened and the almost unbelievable way so many of these victims seemed to be able to forgive the perpetrators of their abuse. Over and over I asked how they were able to offer this forgiveness, and over and over they spoke of Ubuntu.

Nelson Mandela also pointed to the influence of Ubuntu in both finding his calling and forgiving his captors. In his auto-biography, *Long Walk to Freedom*, he says that his early childhood internalization of Ubuntu made it impossible for him to enjoy the limited freedom he was allowed as a young attorney with the privileges of education. He realized that the chains on any one of his people were the chains on all of them, and that the chains on all of his people were the chains on him.[8] He felt compelled to serve his people because he knew that he *was* his people, and his people were him. Forgiveness flowed from this same understanding of his fundamental oneness with all South Africans, regardless of their race.

Ubuntu also shaped his vision when, after being installed as president, he focused his energy on trying to make South Africans feel safe enough that they would remain in the country.[9] He believed that if the whites left, South Africa could never be truly free or whole because the whites belonged as much as the blacks. He was convinced, therefore, that the country must remain multi-racial. Ubuntu helped him to understand that wholeness requires the presence and participation of all constituent parts.

The point of Ubuntu is that each of us belongs to all the others because together we are all members of a larger whole. Ubuntu calls each of us to serve the others that form part of that larger whole. This provides the deep sense of community that leads Africans to recoil at the isolation of Western individualism. Ubuntu asserts that identity, health, freedom, and calling are ultimately found only in the larger whole. Ubuntu teaches that together is better than separate because separate is an illusion.

Ubuntu came to Nelson Mandela as a gift of the perennial wisdom tradition. Africans are closer to this tradition and its wisdom than most of us in the West. We tend to dismiss these sorts of collectivist philosophies because we just can't understand them within the framework of our individualistic cultures.[10] And yet by rejecting their wisdom, we make it harder to know the thick web of interconnectedness that the Great Nest of Being offers. And we are forced to try to construct a purpose for life rather than accept the readily available one—loving and serving others as ourselves—that lies at the core of the perennial wisdom tradition.

Purposeful living is indeed possible, but it is most easily discovered when we consent to the flow of life and recognize the larger wholes within which we exist. Once we begin to sense the deep connections that we have to all people—not just to those of our race, gender, sexual orientation, socioeconomic group, political affiliation, or nation—we can begin to experience the meaning and purpose that flow from living life as members of the human family rather than as isolated individuals.

4

Mysteries of Personhood

When asked what most surprised him about people, the Dalai Lama said, "Man sacrifices his health in order to make money. Then he sacrifices money to recuperate his health. And then he is so anxious about the future than he does not enjoy the present, the result being that he does not live in the present or the future; he lives as if he is never going to die, and then he dies having never really lived."[1]

Humans are full of shocking irrationalities and surprising contradictions. Just when we think we know our most predictable friend, he or she expresses an opinion, discloses a bit of personal history, or does something totally out of character. These inconsistencies make us interesting. Just think how boring someone would be if he or she always acted in a thoroughly predictable and consistent manner!

You don't really know much about humans if you think they are predictable. How we have behaved in the past tells us more about how we will behave in the future than any other single factor or set of factors, and yet this still leaves a gaping chasm of unpredictability.

We know, for example, that pedophiles are likely to reoffend, yet some manage to break this pattern. We know that all of us are prone to repeat self-defeating patterns of behavior rather than remembering and dealing with the underlying conflicts associated with them. And yet occasionally we seem capable of breaking into genuine freedom from these inner tyrannies. We know that the most rational of us regularly engage in deeply irrational behavior, that none of us are simply as we appear, and that all of us are victims of self-deception more often than any deception we try to spin for others. In short, humans are a mystery.

Humans defy being reduced to laws of nature. Guided by instinct, animals are much more predictable than humans. After more than a century of modern psychology, it seems apparent that the notion of laws that govern human nature is oxymoronic.

Mystery and Paradox

To be human is to be suspended between the great polarities of our existence. We are dust and breath, matter and spirit, divine DNA and feet of clay, finite and infinite, insignificant and of inestimable significance, body and self, brain and mind, machine and self-consciousness. None of these things can ever be reconciled. To be human is to live with the tension of the paradoxes that we are.

It is common to refer to this as a mystery. But let us pause for a moment to consider the nature of mystery. From the perspective of the natural sciences, mystery is nothing more than a gap in knowledge. However, the mysteries of personhood are not simply things we don't yet understand. They reflect dimensions of human existence that should not be expected to ever fully yield to rational or scientific analysis. Things like consciousness, the self, imagination, intuition, suffering, birth, and death are saturated with questions that must be lived, not answered. They invite us to engage our humanity more deeply so that we may live our lives more fully and passionately.

The mysteries of personhood—and of life itself—involve tensions between seeming contradictions. Given the binary nature of the default operating system of the human mind, we want to believe that one side of this contradiction must be true and the other false. But the nature of truth can often be grasped only by holding in tension things that seem incompatible with one another and by placing the contradictory elements within a larger perspective.

Paradox is the name for these apparent contradictions. Both sides of the apparent contradiction are true, but both are also only partial truths. What we need to see is the larger truth that contains both of the partial truths. Once again, it is only when we start with the whole that the part-wholes make any sense. The paradoxes and mysteries of humans must be embraced, and the tension generated by doing so must be held if they are to yield their secrets and help us to understand the larger truths of being human.

Parts and Wholes

Many aspects of human personhood seem to pull us in opposite directions until we see them in light of the larger whole within which they both play a crucial role in making us who we are. The conscious and unconscious dimensions of personhood are a good example.

I recently had a conversation with someone who, discovering that I was a psychologist who was interested in spirituality, tried to draw me into an argument over religion. He expressed his hostility to religion at a pretty high level, but after he saw that I wasn't rising to the challenge of an argument, his belligerence began to soften. Almost confidentially he added that the only thing that stood in the way of him believing everything that he had been arguing against was what dreams suggested about the nature of the unconscious. He said that he had based his life on rationality but that this was being challenged by what he was learning in therapy from his dreams. No longer able to dismiss them, he began to wonder whether his whole vision of life had been overly shaped by the conscious dimensions of mind. He wondered whether the things he despised in life—religion was near the top of the list—might look quite different from the perspective of the unconscious, a perspective he was being forced to take more seriously.

I was quite impressed with this man's honesty and openness. Beneath his bluster was a striking receptivity to the challenge he felt that dreams were presenting to his worldview. He was much more open to life than he first appeared. Now he had my interest. I asked him whether there was a particular dream that had challenged his worldview. This is how he answered.

Four months ago I woke one morning with my heart racing and my palms sweaty. But it hardly felt like I was awake. I felt like I was still in the dream, and yet, looking around, I knew I was awake. But everything felt different. And that was what frightened me.

The central character of the dream was a woman I would not normally even notice. The setting was sometime in the past, probably in Europe, although I couldn't tell. When I first saw her she was walking through a palace of some sort. I watched her as she wandered the halls looking at the art. She stopped as she came to a picture of a group of men looking at a cadaver that was being cut open by a figure in black. At the foot of the cadaver was a textbook of some sort. The dead man was as white as a ghost. Suddenly, he sat up and turned to the men who were watching and said something in a language that they didn't seem to understand. Looking puzzled, they turned to the woman standing in front of the picture and asked her if she knew what the corpse said. She said, "What you seek is not to be found here but in what you have rejected." Suddenly the men became very upset and starting arguing quite violently with each other. The corpse ignored them and simply got off the table and walked out of the room. And the woman turned away from the picture, and with a smile on her face, walked out of the room and the house.

Following her down the street, I saw her next enter an old church. I did the same, but once I was inside, I was more interested in the church than the woman. Now I was the one wandering around looking at the statues, art, and architecture. I was fascinated by everything I saw. Walking along a side aisle, I suddenly saw the woman I had been following and noticed that she was again standing in front of what looked like a painting. I couldn't see it very clearly from where I stood, so I decided to go closer. As I did, she walked away, and I saw that what she had been looking at was nothing more than a frame with bare wall behind it. Below the frame was a sign with the words the woman had spoken in the last scene—"What you seek is not to be found here but in what you have rejected." This disturbed me deeply, and I ran after the woman to ask her if she knew what this meant. But I couldn't find her. I then ran out of the church and into the street, and I immediately woke up in a cold sweat. My heart was pounding, and my head ached. I wrote down the details of the dream hoping that would help me set it aside, but all that day the dream haunted me. I still remember it as clearly as if I had just awakened from it. It's a dream that still in some ways haunts me.

Dreams represent a remarkable cooperation between the unconscious and conscious parts of the mind. Arising from within the unconscious, they bring information that is important for our wholeness. This man was still trying to figure out the significance of this dream, and his therapist was wise enough to refrain from telling him what that might be. The fact that it left the man feeling that his world was in a degree of imbalance means that the dream had already worked its primary purpose. It invited him to pause for soulful reflection on the dream and his life, particularly what was missing. Up to this point in the man's life, he had prized reason and the scientific method and had rejected everything that seemed in tension with it. The dream was an invitation to reclaim the dimensions of his self that he had rejected because they did not fit with the self he wished to be.[2]

Easily ignored because they seem so illogical, dreams follow their own logic. Think of it as psycho-logic, the thought process of the unconscious. It is built around symbols instead of words and organized in ways that communicate more indirectly than the ways of consciousness. The unconscious mind tells stories while the conscious mind lists propositions. At times, the unconscious communicates without the support of even a narrative, simply prodding us to action or making us aware of things that are missing from consciousness. Once we begin to learn the language of the unconscious, we discover that this form of communicating is an incredibly rich supplement to consciousness.

Since Freud, it has been common for pop psychology to present the conscious and unconscious dimensions of mind in terms of an iceberg. The 10 percent or so of the iceberg that is above the surface of the water is supposedly consciousness, and the remaining 90 percent that is below the surface is supposedly unconsciousness. But if we ignore the percentages and the implications of one level being more important than the other, what is depicted in this image is quite true to the basic message of depth psychology.[3] The important point of the iceberg image is that both consciousness and unconsciousness form parts of the human mind, which is an integral whole. We do not have two quite different minds but one larger, whole mind that includes the rich contributions of both parts. Both consciousness and the unconscious play a crucial role in human creativity, love, problem solving, play, and much more. Decision making is greatly improved when we know how to include the data from both consciousness and the unconscious. And life can be lived more fully and deeply when it draws from both spheres of the whole mind.[4]

When we look closely at thought and emotion, we see that they also are more integrally connected as parts of a larger whole than we usually realize. Recent neuropsychological research disputes the popular notion that emotions are the enemy of rationality. Emotions now appear to be vital to higher cognitive functioning and essential to good judgment. People with brain damage that impairs their ability to respond emotionally to the content of their thoughts experience gross defects of planning, judgment, and social appropriateness.[5] Evidently, unlike oil and water, emotions and reason do mix quite well together. Decisions that are informed by both emotion and reason appear to be the best because each forms an integral part of the whole psyche. Like consciousness and the unconscious, they are complementary parts of a larger whole, to which they both make a crucial contribution.

Understanding the relationship of parts to the larger whole plays an equally important role in making sense of the mysteries of human identity. Most of us go through most of our lives identifying ourselves by the same name (with slight variations) and with a core of enduring personality traits, a relatively stable identity, and a sense of continuity of the self we think of as "me." But those suffering from dissociative identity disorders lack this stability of self, and what we learn from them helps us to see that for all of us, the self is much more a family of selves than a single entity. We may not have multiple distinct identities that alternately take control of us, but all of us have some degree of the same dissociative tendencies. All of us have parts of self that are unknown to and unwelcome in the larger family of self.

Jung called these the shadow dimensions of self—the parts of self we often have some vague sense of being present but definitely do not want to acknowledge. We may judge them to be weaker than we wish to be, possibly more needy or vulnerable. Or it may be their aggressiveness, sexual freedom, playfulness, innocence, or risk taking that frightens us. For one reason or another, they represent a way of being that we simply reject. However, each of these parts belongs in the larger whole that is the self. Each has a valuable contribution to make to the integral wholeness that we are.

Talk about true and false selves obscures the nature of this larger wholeness that must always include everything that exists within it. These terms play to our primitive binary mind and set us up for either/or thinking and responding. The truth of the self is the whole self. If we attempt to eliminate the rejected parts, they simply increase in their power to keep us fragmented. Wholeness comes from inclusion, not rejection. Only when all the parts of us are welcomed to the table in the family room of the self do we ever have any chance of being the whole person that we truly are.

Freedom and Bondage

Another paradoxical dimension of human personhood that becomes more intelligible when examined from the perspective of the whole is the extent of human freedom. Our inner sense of this matter is that we are free to make choices. In this moment, for example, I feel that I could either continue typing or stop. If I choose to take a break, it feels like I could choose to have a snack, get a drink of water, or take a walk.

That seems simple and clear enough, but what if I am an alcoholic and face the decision whether to make that drink an alcoholic one? Do I still have the same degree of freedom? Or what if I have a long-standing habit of daily use of pornography to avoid boredom? How much freedom of choice do I really have when I decide to go to my computer and visit my favorite porn sites? What if I am trying to lose weight and face the decision about whether to have a late-night snack or whether to go to the fitness center on Saturday morning instead of staying in bed? Or what if I am a pedophile? How much freedom do I have when I try to resist acting on my urges and impulses? These questions are obviously not merely of academic concern—at least they won't be to anyone who has honestly faced addictive patterns in either their behavior or the behavior of those they love or live with.

With freedom comes responsibility. In the absence of freedom, the case for responsibility is considerably weakened. But while we sometimes think of freedom in terms of whether an act is voluntary and committed while the person is capable of choice, the binary nature of this question should warn us that we are approaching the matter in an oversimplified manner. It should alert us to the fact that we need to step back and take a more holistic perspective.

With human behavior, the whole that we need to consider starts with the whole history of choices related to the behaviors in question. All human actions have consequences. One consequence of the choices we make is that they will either increase or decrease our future freedom. Let me give a dramatic example to illustrate a point that is less easily seen but equally true in much less dramatic choices. Let's assume that you have total freedom the first time you use crack cocaine.[6] That freedom will be rapidly reduced by each subsequent decision to use the drug, which is the reason we speak of crack as a highly addictive drug.

Clearly we all have a history of choices that influences our freedom in the present. The striking reality is that whatever present limitations we experience, the choices we make within them will either increase or decrease our bondage.

It is, however, possible to claw our way back to increased freedom in relation to our most destructive behaviors. It may be an extremely long, hard road, and we may never come to the same degree of freedom that we had when we took the first steps in the direction that led to our bondage. But at every point in human life, our choices either increase or decrease freedom.

I say this after years of work with people who were caught in cycles of extremely destructive behavior. I have watched children go from torturing animals to adolescents who kill humans for the thrill of doing so. Crack addicts may lack the freedom to choose whether to take a hit when the effects of the last hit have worn off, but they retain the freedom to choose to get help. Pedophiles usually start with a history of sexual abuse, but how they respond to this quickly begins to increase or decrease future degrees of freedom. In a domain of human functioning that is as resistant to change as any we know of, I have seen how choices in the present can allow the pedophile who is genuinely motivated to do the necessary but extremely hard inner work to recover some capacity for choice and control.

But there is another dimension of the larger whole that must also be included in increasing inner freedom. Willpower is not enough to reverse the most serious forms of the bondages we choose. We need the help of other people who are part of the larger whole within which we exist. When we battle addictive dynamics on our own, we will almost always lose the battle. In the case of significant losses of freedom, we can't drag ourselves out of bondage simply by willpower and resolve alone. We are fooling ourselves if we think we can.

There are many reasons why twelve-step programs are as integral to any addiction treatment approach as they are, but one of the most important reasons is that they demand that addicts abandon their secrecy and isolation and join the community of fellow addicts. In truth, what they are joining is the human community. All humans live with the same recognized or unrecognized addictive dimensions of their lives. We differ only in the social acceptability of our addictions and our willingness to name them for what they are. However, we are truly capable of gaining freedom from the most pernicious of our addictions only when we do so as members of a community. And the more that community grounds us in our humanity and increases our solidarity with all other humans, the greater the chances are of restoring the freedom we have squandered by past choices. The route to genuine freedom is the route to deep and meaningful embeddedness within larger wholes and bigger causes. This is the context within which we find the freedom and purpose of a meaningful life.

Good and Evil

One of the most paradoxical things about humans is that our enormous capacity for generosity and selfless love is matched by an equally astounding capacity for cruelty, greed, and destructiveness. To be human is to carry within us the seeds of great good and great evil, great light and great darkness, great creativity and great destructiveness. While humans have produced the art of the Sistine Chapel, the music that fills the world's concert halls, and the pyramids of Egypt, in the last one hundred years we have also committed acts of genocide and mass murder that resulted in the deaths of over 250 million people.[7] For every Nelson Mandela or Mahatma Gandhi, we have at least one Joseph Stalin, Adolf Hitler, or Pol Pot. For every person who squanders his or her life on spreading love, we have those who destroy their own lives and those of countless others as they spread hatred and destruction.

Philosophers and theologians have usually referred to this as the problem of evil. They could, of course, have called it the problem of good. But whether one starts by assuming that human nature is good, evil, or both, it is hard to ignore the tension that exists between good and evil. Like oil and water, they do not seem to go together. It is hard to imagine a larger whole that could contain them both and make it easier to hold the tension of this paradoxical dimension of humanity.

Again, it is tempting to think of this in binary terms and conclude that the world can be divided into good people and bad people. In the extremes, the classification may seem to work. But it involves a dangerous distortion of reality because the capacity for both good and evil lies within each of us. A failure to recognize our own insipient darkness merely sets us up to project it onto others. As we have already seen, refusing to acknowledge the existence of inner darkness does not eliminate it but actually increases the probability that it will tyrannize us. This is a fundamental operating principle of the unconscious. It is also the reason why our freedom can come only from naming and embracing the unwelcome parts of self, gathering them all up together so they can make their contribution to the whole self we truly are.

I recognize, however, that this strategy might sound naive when it comes to evil. Even if you are willing to agree that the capacity for evil exists in all of us, perhaps you feel that the best strategy for dealing with evil is containment. But such an approach fails to understand the psychology of evil.

Any adequate understanding of evil must engage both the existential and personal levels of analysis. No one has offered a more penetrating discussion of the existential grounds of evil than Ernest Becker.[8] His argument is that the root of human evil is our avoidance of the anxiety and sense of vulnerability associated with our mortality. We attempt to escape awareness of our existential vulnerability and gain self-esteem through the achievement of a heroic self-image. Society helps to bolster this denial of death by offering what Becker calls "immortality systems"—groups and causes that inflate us with a sense of invulnerable righteousness. But having aligned ourselves with one of these absolute-truth systems we then must protect ourselves against the challenge that comes from other such systems. To do so we attack and degrade the adherents of other absolute-truth systems as a way to defend against the anxiety and sense of vulnerability associated with our mortality.

But even if we accept the validity of this analysis, personal psychology also has a role to play in fostering evil. Evil isn't a trait. Neither is it a psychopathology or a failure of moral development. Once again, it is a consequence of choices. No one is born evil. Neither is evil simply the inevitable result of things that happen to us. Evil may have roots in our personal histories, and the capacity for evil may be inherent in human nature, but what brings evil into existence is the choices we make—primarily, choices about the way we respond to the things that happen to us.

The soil out of which a mass murderer or serial sex offender develops is unhealed emotional wounds. Almost always these wounds are caused by recurring, not simply isolated, incidents. Usually this involves long-term and repeated sexual, physical, and emotional abuse. Often it involves systematic torture. But again, it is not the fact of this abuse but the way the person responds to it that makes the difference. I have worked with children and adults who experienced years of torture and unbelievable levels of sadistic cruelty who were able to experience inner healing that allowed them to move on in life with remarkable inner freedom and well-being. But when these wounds are left raw, the only recourse is to protect our vulnerability by externalizing the toxicity that has been internalized. And this is exactly what we see happening in the lives of people who commit acts that are judged to be evil.

In addition to a profound sense of loss and excruciating levels of vulnerability, the other most frequent consequence of such wounds is rage. When nursed rather than released, this rage inevitably begins to spill into behavior that will increasingly become overtly hostile. Although we sometimes think of expressing anger as a way to drain it off, the expression of anger empowers us and distances us from the vulnerability of the original emotional wounds. This empowerment can be quite addictive, and expressing it can strengthen rather than lessen our rage.

But anger—even murderous rage—is not the same as evil. Evil is shaped in response to love. Anger that gets transformed into evil is anger that people have chosen to embrace with love. They love their rage. Usually it is the only thing they love. Experiencing their own woundedness as betrayals of love, they chose to turn away from human love. This is what I mean when I speak of evil being formed in response to love. This love of their hatred is a choice, though it may be unconscious and is certainly far from wholly free. It is a response to their woundedness that reinforces their developing vulnerability to evil. When anger is embraced it quickly turns into hatred that leaves no room for anyone else in our life.

Loving our anger isn't the same as accepting it as a part of our self. Loving our anger is a perversion of love. With great willfulness, hatred is clutched as our most precious possession. It alone seems to hold the key to the possibility of rising beyond powerlessness. It alone seems to hold the potential of helping the person to make a difference, be noticed, and be taken seriously. This is how small, angry people like Hitler and Stalin overcome their chronic feelings of inferiority and attempt to be noticed and taken seriously. And it is the same dynamic that we see in teens who take bags of ammunition and automatic weapons into schools with the intent of indiscriminately killing as many people as they can.

There is no simple way to prevent these sorts of evil acts. But we must remember that it is wounded, fearful people who harm others. The path of prevention is the path of healing and the cultivation of courageous awareness of our basic existential vulnerability. The first part of this involves something we need to undertake as societies, while the second is something we need to do as individuals.

The first thing we need to do is to take some of the money we pour into making prisons and use it instead to fund universally accessible, quality mental health treatment programs. Building prisons plays to fears; treatment moves upstream and seeks to prevent the utterly destructive things we fear—things that presently cost us as societies so much more than we will ever spend on their prevention.

At a more personal level, the path of preventing our own potential evil is, as we have seen already, the path of welcoming the unwelcome parts of self to the family of self. This act of hospitality is as applicable in relation to the big issues of evil as it is to any other dimension of human personhood. If the wounded, vulnerable self is welcomed, it never gets a chance to grow into the hostile, powerless self, which is much more dangerous. Not only can the healing of our woundedness and the anger and powerlessness associated with it come from welcoming these parts of self, but this is also the only way in which our anger and vulnerability can ever make their essential contribution to the whole selves we truly are. Every bit of our experience and every level of our being are needed for our wholeness. But the various strands cannot be woven together and aligned with the whole until they are welcomed as guests in the guesthouse of our being.

However, in addition to this we also need to address the existential taproot of evil—our avoidance of the reality of death. We need to free ourselves from the cultural network of lies that ward off the awareness of mortality. And we need the courage to speak the truth about the human condition and face the precariousness and fragility of our existence. It is only after we fully accept the reality of our eventual death and embrace the vulnerability of living in its light that we can place our full trust in the ground of our being and nest of our ultimate belonging.

Before we leave the mystery of how humans can be capable of both great good and great evil, I want to say one more thing about evil. In my opinion, evil is an adjective that should be applied to deeds, not people. Getting to know even a relatively small number of people widely characterized as evil, but getting to know them extremely well, has made it impossible for me to call them evil. Things simply look different when viewed through empathy. People sometimes ask me whether anything surprises me after decades of work as a psychotherapist, much of it as a forensic psychologist. The answer is no. But the reason for that is not desensitization but the empathy that comes from being able to know the big picture of the person's whole life and experience. Nothing shocks me once I understand it in the context of a person's life. And if I am honest, I am forced to acknowledge that given the same history and life context I could easily make choices that could lead me to the same place.

What, then, is the essence of evil? Perhaps evil is simply actions and inner postures that are antilife. Maybe this is also the essence of what theologians call "sin." If so, it is clear that we can locate low levels of this antilife orientation much further upstream than the actual acts that appear so obviously evil. That being the case, the early choices that turn us away from life should be understood as the precursors of evil. Once again, we are brought back to the consequences of our choices.

Feet of Clay and Divine DNA

But perhaps these various paradoxical mysteries of being human are best seen in a still larger perspective. When we return to the Great Nest of Being, we can recall the way in which it spans what we perceive to be the gulf between dust and divinity. However, the levels of existence that are suggested by the perennial wisdom tradition are not simply five planks that form a bridge between these two sides of a chasm. They are components of a dynamic spiral that reflects the way in which we move through various levels of being as we weave ever more intimately together the matter and spirit that form the essence of our being.

The wisdom tradition reminds us that this synthesis of matter, life, mind, soul, and spirit is our most essential nature and destiny. To be human is to have both feet of clay and divine DNA. Depending on which way you look at it, you could describe us as inspirited matter or embodied spirit. We are a synthesis of matter and spirit.

We tend to focus on only one side of this framework and ignore the other. Humanists and New Age religionists focus on our divine DNA. They remind us of our enormous value and potential. Others tend to focus more on our feet of clay, reminding us of our frailty, weakness, and, in some cases, what they consider to be our essential "badness." Typically, neither group provides us with the whole picture. It is only in placing matter and spirit together with life, mind, and soul that we can understand the big picture. And that picture is the dynamic spiral of existence—a spiral that eternally draws everything from matter, life, mind, soul, and spirit together and weaves it into integral wholeness.

But we do not lose our feet of clay when we embrace our divine DNA. Even when we transcend a lower level of being, it remains an integral part of us. In chapter 2 I said that each level of existence enfolds all lower levels. Transformation is development that starts with envelopment. To be human will always—regardless of how enlightened or whole we become—involve living with both feet of clay and divine DNA.

This spiral of existence is the great nest of human existence. This is our source and our destiny. We must, therefore, resist being drawn into reductionistic accounts of human being—what we might call "nothing but" accounts. We are not just matter. Neither are we just life, just mind, just soul, or just spirit. We are the cosmic dance of all five—a dance that plays itself out in every cell of our being just as much as it does in every corner of the cosmos. That is what it means to live the mystery of personhood!

5

Ego-Based Being

To be human is to possess a great lightness of being. Too often we are aware only of the weight of our lives and have no sense of the buoyancy of our essential self. But being—human being in particular—contains an expansive weightlessness that can be noticed when we step outside our preoccupations and have enough stillness to be present to our existence.

If you have been attentive, you may recall moments in your life when you sensed something of this lightness of being. While it was probably just for an instant, in that moment you glimpsed something of the vastness of the soul's interior horizon. Perhaps you felt caught up in its spaciousness, awed by its expansiveness, maybe even terrified by its emptiness. The core of your experience, however, was probably a sense of euphoria and interconnectedness, which was likely complemented by overtones of profound well-being, awe, integration, and harmony. Abraham Maslow called this state of consciousness a "peak experience." Others have described it as "cosmic consciousness." It is quite distant from the normal state of consciousness most of us live with for much of our lives,

Mari Carmen

71

but it is an important reference point to keep in mind as we focus in this chapter on the default state of being. Without these moments, we might never know that anything else is possible.

Listening to our great myths can help us stay in touch with this lightness of being. We have already noted how the Judeo-Christian creation story captures this lightness in the metaphorical description of humans as the dust of the earth, vitalized by the breath of God.[1] The sacred Taoist text *T'ai Shang Ch'ing-ching Ching* uses a similar metaphor, describing humans as created from the descent of heavenly breath and the ascent of earthly vapor.[2] Both recognize the fundamental insubstantiality of human existence—dust and vapor are both easily blown away by too much breath or a gust of wind!

The mystics are most aware of and, at the same time, the least threatened by the lightness of their being. Indeed, they have learned to delight in it. Hildegard von Bingen described herself as a feather on the breath of God.[3] Her sense of lightness of being was a profound comfort to her because rather than feeling blown around by every gust of wind, she experienced herself as being borne on the breath of her Beloved. Without this sense of being safely held within some larger whole, lightness of being will not bring spaciousness and possibilities of buoyancy. It will bring only a sense of vulnerability. The primary way in which we defend against this vulnerability is to shift our center from our naked, vulnerable, and insubstantial self to our ego, which appears to have more substance. Unfortunately, that substance is not only more apparent than real, but it also restricts our freedom and enormously diminishes our lightness of being. While this may lessen the sense of threat, it deepens our disconnection from the larger wholes within which we find the ultimate relief from our vulnerability.

In order to understand the significance of this shift of our center from the self to the ego and the way in which this shapes consciousness, we need to step back for a moment to look more carefully at what we call "consciousness." It is time to get better acquainted with it if we are to understand the way in which consciousness works with ego to shape our default mental operating system, which I will be calling "the egoic mind."

Human and Cosmic Consciousness

In the West, we tend to think of consciousness as a human property or, more specifically, as a by-product of the brain of individual humans. However, this sort of anthropocentric, materialistic, and individualistic thinking is not what we see in the East. Hindu and Buddhist philosophers have long argued that consciousness pervades the universe. Its primary home is the cosmos, where it serves as the glue that holds everything that exists together. Individual personal consciousness is simply a drop in this cosmic sea of consciousness. As our personal consciousness expands, however, the mystics say that we can knowingly participate in this larger consciousness, which is described variously as "the cosmic Christ" (Christianity), *satori* (Zen), or Indra's net (Buddhism). Regardless of how it is named or understood, this is the tightly woven web within which everything that exists is held.

We see something of this transpersonal understanding of consciousness in Carl Jung's notion of the collective unconscious, which he described as a sort of divine energy that permeates the universe. Teilhard de Chardin also viewed consciousness in cosmic and energetic terms, describing it as a force that combines but transcends the powers of mind, spirit, and love. It is the animating and awakening energy that lies behind, underneath, and ahead of us at all times. Learning to inhabit this ultimate whole in which we already exist is the goal of all human unfolding and becoming.

This concept of cosmic consciousness would be nothing but interesting speculation if it were not for the fact that many people report experiences in which they sense they have tapped into this larger, transpersonal state of consciousness. These experiences come as sudden and intense feelings of well-being that are often tinged with wonder and awe. When describing these moments, people often speak of feeling as if they had, for a moment, been snatched out of themselves and allowed to experience life from a self-transcendent perspective. Often the beauty of nature, great art, or music triggers these moments. They can emerge in the most surprising contexts and can produce changes that are long lasting and noticeable to others.[4]

Even more than a *state* of consciousness (that is, a transient experience), cosmic consciousness is also a potential *level* of consciousness (i.e., a stable platform from which life can be viewed and experienced).[5] Listen to the experience of one such person who shared her experience with me as she sought to understand the significance of what she knew as a stable part of her normal state of consciousness.

> I don't like to be seen as special in any way apart from the special-ness that comes from being an ordinary woman. But I do seem to have been blessed with a clear and strong sense of the unity of all things. I read books that talk about non-dual consciousness, and they describe something that I have always known. Where others see trees, I see a forest and know I am part of it. Where others seem to see only the sun or the moon, I see the universe and know that it is within me and I am within it. I hear harmony, not individual notes. I can't understand how it could be otherwise. I sense wholeness, not fragmentation. I don't understand when I hear people talk about trying to know the presence of God. I can't imagine what it would be like to not know this presence as my most fundamental reality. What are others missing? Or am I deluding myself? And when people speak about trying to find God, I am confused. The God I know is so deeply part of me, and I am so deeply part of this God, that I can no longer see the point of separateness or distinction. I sometimes worry that this means that something is dreadfully wrong with me, but I wouldn't give up what I know for anything. I just couldn't stand the sense

of aloneness that must go with not knowing that I belong within and am part of everything that is.

This woman isn't crazy. She came to me because she was concerned she might be and felt she needed a professional opinion from a clinical psychologist. But she was as sane as anyone I have ever met. Free from any diagnosable psychopathology, she had strong ego boundaries and a great deal of psychological health and maturity. She did not live life in a psychotic fog of enmeshment. She had not lost contact with reality, and neither was her contact with reality slipping. What she was experiencing was understandable tension between her own deep knowing of the interconnectedness of everything that exists and the culturally supported illusion of the separate, disconnected self. What she was experiencing was an astounding gift of knowing her place in the Great Nest of Being.

While only a small percentage of humans experience this as a stable state of consciousness, the fact that some do tells us something very important about the possibilities of human becoming. I believe it tells us that human consciousness is possible only because we are the progeny of a conscious universe. If consciousness did not first exist in the cosmos, it could not be part of human existence. Humans don't possess consciousness so much as participate in it. Expansion of consciousness involves tapping more and more into the larger pool of cosmic consciousness. The way in which we do this is through openness and emptiness. An absence of either of these prerequisites constricts the flow of consciousness and shows itself as egoic self-preoccupation.

In summary, human consciousness can be described as the space within which our awareness of things arises as we tap into the larger pool of cosmic consciousness. It is the platform on which we stand as we engage with the phenomena of both the inner and outer worlds. Consciousness provides our framework for organizing experience and determines our way of being in the world. It is, therefore, the core of our identity, since identity and consciousness are inextricably intertwined in humans. How we understand and relate to ourselves reflects and shapes how we experience everything that is beyond our selves.

As I mentioned earlier, one of the tasks of consciousness is to organize awareness and equip us to engage with reality. This task begins to sound overwhelming when we remember that human consciousness taps into the fundamental cosmic energy and glue that moves everything forward while also holding everything together. This is where the ego enters the picture. Ego specializes in organizing the roiling array of reality that consciousness accesses. It does this by keeping things simple—something it does extremely well.

Ego and Egocentricity

Recently it has become popular among people who approach the inner life and its transformation from a spiritual perspective to treat ego as the great enemy of spirit. This is unfortunate because, in truth, ego plays an indispensable role in both human being and becoming. It deserves a much better reputation than it tends to have in spiritual circles in the West.

Much of the reason for ego bashing arises from the confusion of ego and egocentricity. Egocentricity is a defense against the narcissistic injuries that we inevitably experience while growing up. These injuries are anything that threaten our sense of well-being or diminish our feelings of self-worth. It is our way of trying to protect the ego from further damage. Egocentricity is the bandage we wrap around our self-esteem when it feels fragile. Rather than being a mark of an ego that is too strong, egocentricity is a mark of a fragile and vulnerable ego. But when the bandage is wrapped too tightly, it cuts us off from the source of life. That source of life is not ego. It is the self as it exists within the larger whole in which it belongs.[6]

Ego allows us to perceive, organize, elaborate, differentiate, integrate, and transform experience. It also secures our reality testing, good judgment, impulse control, defensive functions, affective regulation, interpersonal relations, moral orientation, thought processes, and much more. But it takes a strong and mature ego to accomplish all these tasks. For that reason, many people who seek spiritual transformation often need to step back and do more basic psychological work before they are ready for the spiritual work that attracts them. Psychotherapy aimed at ego strengthening and maturation is often a necessary precursor to spiritual direction or transformational coaching that seeks to help people transcend the ego. Nothing can be transcended until it is integrated.

While the contours of ego are present at birth, it takes decades to cultivate the necessary ego strength to allow a person to eventually transcend ego and know the spaciousness of being. Ego development does not happen automatically with the passage of time; it cannot be rushed, and it is indispensable for both human being and becoming. Quite simply, without ego there can be no self, and without a self, there can be no transformation. In order to plumb the depths of transformation that become uniquely possible in the second half of life, the development of a sufficiently strong and flexible ego in the first half is crucial.

The ego is partial and frail, but it believes itself to be whole and absolute. Its favorite cognitive strategy is to emphasize difference rather than sameness. Consequently, it is a master of establishing boundaries and making comparisons and distinctions. Although it operates at both an unconscious and conscious level, the ego focuses on conscious thoughts to the exclusion of other dimensions and levels of being. As a result, the ego-self is isolated, and ego consciousness is preoccupied with mental contents (particularly thoughts) and our body. Cut off from the heart, ego leaves us in a place of isolated individuality—a fragment of a branch broken from the tree that is our true place of belonging.

The Binary Brain and the Default Mental Operating System

The ego's most essential role is to help us organize internal and external realities. While this is a huge task, the ego is uniquely equipped to handle it by means of a remarkably powerful tool— the binary brain. Binary thinking did not arise out of advances in computer technology. Rather, computer algorithms were developed to mirror the way the binary brain works. We ourselves gave birth to the computer age because it was already in us!

The human brain is the most complicated organ in the universe, but its basic architecture is extremely simple. In crude terms, we can think of it as a network of off/on switches that are connected by short pieces of wire with a very small gap between each wire and the next. The 86 billion neurons that make up the average human brain serve as electrical conductors.[7] Basically, we can think of them as the wire. Energy flows in only one direction down these short pieces of wire, and the switch at the end of each controls whether the signal gets transmitted across the gap between it and the next wire. Messages that get transmitted across this gap are carried by neurotransmitters that tell the next cluster of neurons either to fire or not. All neural messages are reducible to simple binary codes of either zero or one, off or on. But out of that simplicity emerges the enormous complexity that makes up the human brain, which in turn supports human access of cosmic consciousness.

How does the ego make use of this binary brain? The default operating system that seems to be installed in us at birth runs on the power of either/or.[8] Not only is this sort of processing what the brain does best, but it also suits the work of the ego to keep things simple. The ego's role is to organize complex data and simplify it by reducing it into basic polar opposites, an ability that we now know is built in to the very structure of the human brain.[9]

In this binary mental mode, everything gets divided, classified, and compared. Everything that the egoic mind knows, it knows by means of comparison. This is a strategy to make sense of the world by simplifying it—dividing reality into categories such as inside/outside, subject/object, pleasant/unpleasant, win/lose, or other such dualistic distinctions. With practice we no longer even notice that we are making these binary judgments. At a glance we feel we can accurately identify whether people are like us, are successful or a failure, are worthy of respect, are to be feared, are attractive, and much more. And once people are separated, classified, and compared in this way, it is almost impossible to resist the tendency to also judge them as good or not good.

Binary classification systems are not bad per se—at least not when we are young and immature. They can be very helpful in the first half of life because they simplify the complexities of existence. But simplification distorts reality by forcing it to fit into two categories when most of life falls outside whatever two boxes we might try to force it into. Judgments are simply a way to distance ourselves from people, things, and ideas that we reject out of fear, defensiveness, or a fragile sense of superiority.

Ego-Shaped Identity and Consciousness

The most unfortunate consequence of this egoic way of dividing reality into binary bits is the way this shapes identity and consciousness. Under the influence of ego and the default operating system of consciousness, identity forms around uniqueness, not sameness. We begin to see ourselves as a collection of distinctive attributes, and as we look at others, we see them in terms of how they are similar to and different from us. Life is experienced through this binary filter, and the result is dualistic consciousness.

But just as we tend to forget that we are seeing through a filter while we are wearing polarizing sunglasses, so too we are blissfully unaware that we see life through a dualistic filter. We assume that what we see is what is really there. That is the nature of consciousness. We trust our perception and the subsequent quick judgments that neatly chop the world into binary bits we can manage. But the great spiritual traditions have always taught that what we see is a mirage. They have always said that seeing life through a dualistic filter draws us into a grand illusion because our perceptions are not good representations of external reality.

Ego simply cannot grasp wholes. Its default strategy is to divide complexities to make them manageable. But larger wholes are indivisible, which makes them a threat to ego, since it has only one tool. As the saying goes, if all you have is a hammer, every problem looks like a nail. If all you have is ego, everything looks like an ego problem that can be neatly dealt with in terms of either/ or binary judgments.

The larger truths that contain both of the partial truths that the binary mind presents us with are incomprehensible to egoic consciousness. Egoic consciousness simply cannot provide us with the tools we need to deal with contradictions, paradoxes, and mystery. Remember, its specialty is keeping things neat and simple!

However, ego shapes consciousness in yet another way. Ego is the center of the conscious mind, around which we organize everything else. But as this happens, we lose contact with the wholeness that includes both the conscious and unconscious elements of our being. We also lose contact with our heart, our spirit, and our soul. What we are most in contact with is our thoughts, which form our primary identification and become the almost constant background of our consciousness.

Most people are so completely identified with the voice in their head and the emotions that accompany this soundtrack that one might say they are possessed by their mind. They relate to the thinker of the thoughts that fill their default state of consciousness as their essential self. To describe this self as egoic does not mean that it is narcissistic in the usual sense of that word. It simply reflects the fact that every thought is self-referential; it's all about "me." If we were really listening, we would quickly realize that the soundtrack is unbelievably boring. Over and over it repeats the same short loop of *my* opinions, *my* grievances, *my* preferences, *my* latest obsessions, *my* frustrations, *my* needs, *my* plans, *my* anxieties, *my* desires, *my* interpretation of recent events, and on and on. While this state of being may meet the minimalist Cartesian criterion—"I think, therefore I am"—it would be closer to the truth if we finished this sentence by adding one more word: "I think, therefore I am *asleep*!" Like the monotonous and repetitive voice of a hypnotist, this soundtrack lulls us into a state of unconsciousness.

A Portrait of the Egoic Self

I don't mean to be unkind, but the easiest way to get a portrait of the egoic self is to look in a mirror. That is certainly true for me. No matter how much we move beyond it, our egoic self remains part of our inner landscape. So even if it doesn't show its face very clearly to others, it certainly will be quite easy to spot if we are prepared to be honest.

The self that is shaped by the egoic mind has a number of stable characteristics. At the core is the need to compare, classify, and separate our selves from others who we feel are not like us. Swirling about this core is the resulting tendency to complain, resent, and envy. All of these ways of being are so fundamental to the egoic self that they feel normal. But while they may be the norm for this default level of self-organization, they are far from being our most essential self.

Just when I think I have finally left behind my tendency to define myself by who I am not, I notice that I have again concluded that I am not like someone I dislike. If I meet an annoyingly rigid and opinionated person, I notice how quickly I hear myself feeling smug satisfaction that I am not, in my not-so-humble opinion, like him or her. Although I don't usually get enough distance from my thoughts to really notice them, I am then likely to hold on to these mental mutterings for an astoundingly long time—sometimes until someone new comes along and annoys me!

How easily we identify ourselves by what and who we *don't* want to be like. Sometimes this is an individual—perhaps a parent, a disliked boss at work, or a partner in a relationship that is going sour. Often, however, the focus of this dis-identification is groups of people who threaten us in some way. Sometimes these prejudices take on religious or ethnic qualities—although, if we have been properly socialized, we quickly learn to be discreet in terms of whom we share these with. In private, however, we might notice judgments about not being like blacks, whites, Jews, Chinese, Muslims, Latinos, or other groups. Again, dis-identification displays the presence of our egoic self.

These sorts of comparisons and subsequent dis-identifications comfort the egoic self. By reducing complexities through simplification, they reduce some of the existential anxiety of living. But beyond these more trivial things, there are even darker dimensions of the egoic self. Comparing and classifying things and people predispose the egoic self to complain about, resent, and envy those who are judged to be not like us.

Complaining is ego's favorite strategy for strengthening itself. In essence, a complaint is a story we make up about what we think we deserve and how we think things ought to be. We may or may not voice this complaint. Often we are content to simply make it part of the inner dialogue that forms the soundtrack of consciousness. But a complaint is the passageway that resentment uses to worm its way into the soul, and once resentment enters as a guest, it quickly makes our place its place.

Resentment provides an even stronger reinforcement for the egoic self than the simple complaint. We feel offended at something done, said, noticed, or imagined. Then we feel angry. There will always be a judgment buried somewhere in this process. We infer someone's dishonesty, insensitivity, hostility, or lack of integrity. Taking this personally, we then become offended and irritated. Sometimes the "fault" we perceive in the other person is in us and is being projected onto them. Other times it may actually be present in the other person, but by focusing on it to the exclusion of everything else, we amplify it. The fault doesn't really matter because reality isn't the issue. The issue is the hungry ghost within us needing to be fed, and that ghost is the egoic self. Resentment feeds the hunger of the egoic self that is cut off from the taproot of sustenance and vitality that our self would otherwise receive from life itself.

All of us have lived life through the filter of the egoic self. Most people spend most of their lives doing so because they don't realize there is any other way. If they notice these features of their egoic self, they simply assume these processes are a fundamental part of being human. But they aren't. The egoic self is simply a way of being when we are cut off from the flow of life pulling us toward an alternate organization of self that already exists within us. In so many ways, the alternate way of being is deeper and truer to our humanity. It is more organic, more integral, more vital, and more life enhancing. It is a way of being that places us firmly within the flow of human becoming. It is the way of the heart.

6

Heart-Based Becoming

As my primary focus shifts from human being to human becoming, perhaps we should pause for a moment to reflect on this concept of becoming before we turn our attention to the heart. If, as we saw in chapter 1, the three properties of everything that has being are oneness, truth, and goodness, what can we say about the nature of becoming? What are its essential properties?

In its simplest terms, becoming involves a realization of potentialities. The direction of becoming moves from potentiality to actuality, from merely being human to becoming fully human. Human becoming does not involve transcending our humanity but fully actualizing it.

The ancient Greek philosopher Heraclitus said that nothing in this world is constant except change and becoming. Everything flows toward the realization of possibilities that are inherent in being. But this is a flow that is easily disrupted.

Mental health professionals sometimes focus on treating psychopathology while failing to pay attention to the way in which it has disrupted development. For example, a child with a social anxiety disorder needs help not simply in feeling less anxious but in reengaging with peers and continuing to develop social skills and all the other competencies that come along with them. Similarly, a person who has been abused and has a diagnosable post-traumatic stress disorder needs not only symptom relief but also help to get back into the developmental flow of life and pick up from where things suddenly ground to a halt. Regaining developmental traction is usually the core of any effective treatment. Once a person begins moving along developmentally, therapy gains traction and effectiveness.

The human journey of becoming can, of course, also be disrupted by other things. Family crises and serious medical problems can also block forward movement and cause regression. This happens to adults as well as children. We easily get caught in the eddies and countercurrents that are often at their strongest close to the shore of fast-flowing rivers. When this happens, we are frequently pulled backward. Teaching someone to swim harder or faster isn't enough. We have to help them get back into the flow of the river so they can be pulled along by the current. We have to teach them that while staying near the shore may feel safe, it blocks them from the benefits of being pulled along by the uninterrupted flow of the river of life.

Humans are pulled forward in this river by two major currents, both of which draw us in the same general direction. One current is developmental, and the other is evolutionary. The developmental current pulls us toward growth—that is, maturation in the various dimensions of self-development, which includes the emotional, moral, aesthetic, interpersonal, cognitive, and a dozen or so other dimensions of the self. The second major current is the evolutionary one. This pulls us toward transformation—that is, changes in the level of our self-organization. Much more than simply a matter of growth or maturation, this involves a reorganization of the self that is expressed in terms of a radical expansion of consciousness and identity.

Both the developmental and evolutionary currents encourage movement in the direction of becoming more than we are—more mature, more conscious, more aligned with the truth of our being, and more whole. Both form part of the great subterranean current of human life I call "becoming."

Being is never a matter of static existence. We are always being gently pulled beyond where we presently are. The reason I speak of heart-shaped becoming is that the heart has a particularly important role to play in our becoming more than we are. It offers us an alternative to the default human operating system that I described as the egoic self in chapter 5. Like any upgraded operating system, it has to be downloaded to be accessed. In this chapter, we will explore how to do this as we reflect together on what it means to trust our hearts and live heart-centered lives. However, before we get to those questions, we must first pause to clarify the nature and importance of the human heart.

The Heart in Science and the Wisdom Tradition

What is this heart that has so much importance for human becoming? My first tendency is to suggest that it is the metaphorical heart that has long been associated with things like courage, compassion, wisdom, love, and much more. But heart science has recently begun to connect the pump in the chest to the metaphorical heart of the wisdom tradition. While all the details of how the physiological and psychospiritual aspects of the heart come together are not yet clear, the literal and the metaphorical understandings of the heart seem to point in the same general direction.

Research on heart rhythms and the physiological mechanisms by which the heart communicates with the brain has begun to make clear how powerfully the physical heart influences not just health but information processing, decision making, perceptions, and emotions.[1] The heart is much more than just an organ in

the circulatory system of the body. By means of the rhythms of
its pumping action, it sends messages throughout the body that
regulate our emotional, spiritual, and physical well-being. Positive
emotions create coherence in heart rhythms, and, quite remarkably,
artificially induced coherence in those rhythms produces corre-
spondingly positive emotions.

We now know that the heart is a highly complex, self-organized
information-processing center with its own functional "brain."
The heart brain communicates with, influences, and is influenced
by the cranial brain in ways that are crucial for human well-being.
Both are part of a larger whole, and this larger whole includes
many of the things that have long been associated with the metaphorical heart of the wisdom tradition.

In the wisdom tradition the heart, not the brain, connects us
to what exists beyond us. The heart has the bigger perspective.
It can see further than the mind because it draws its data from
all levels of reality, including but never limited to the mind. The
heart is our spiritual center because it is the seat of imagination
and intuition. It is the heart that dreams and, through our deepest desires, leads us forward on our journey of unfolding. It is the
heart that senses wholes, "gets" poetry and art, and gives us our
expansiveness—stretching out beyond our individuality to connect
us to the very heart of the universe. Unlike ego, the heart doesn't
perceive by differentiation but by means of its inherent resonance
with wholeness, alignment, oneness, harmony, proportion, and
beauty. Is it any surprise that this heart has long been recognized
in spiritual teaching as the core of our being? This is the heart that
holds both the mysteries and potentialities of human personhood.

Over and over again Jesus emphasized the heart. It determines
everything we do, say, and even think.[2] Jesus taught that it is the
pure in heart who will see God.[3] The heart he was talking about
is the organ of perception that lies at our deepest center. This is
why cleaning the lens of the heart allows us to see and love God.
St. Augustine tells us that the whole purpose of life is to restore

to health the eye of the heart, for it is by the heart that God may be seen and known to be within.[4] In the words of the eighteenth-century Christian theologian William Law, "Turn to thy heart and thy heart will find . . . its God, within itself."[5]

The heart allows us to keep track of important truths that we are unable to grasp with our minds. Its primary function is to help us see and be aligned with our Source, and it accomplishes this function best when it is pure. This purity comes from being undivided, free from the influence of the false self and disordered emotions and desires. When the heart is pure, we can see through it and trust our inner compass, which, when we learn how to read it, will dependably serve as a source of deep inner wisdom.

The heart is the threshold of the transcendent. Through it we find the treasures of heaven. This is why Jesus spoke of guarding our hearts and being careful with what we count to be its treasures, since the supreme treasure of the heart is that it is the residence of the Supreme Reality. The real glory of being human is the glory of what we encounter in our hearts. This is why the purification of the heart is the key to its transformation and why the transformation of the heart—not merely changed beliefs or behaviors—is the essence of human becoming.

Heart and Mind

While the heart is the doorway to the self-transcendent, it is a doorway through which we cannot pass without bringing the mind along. The heart is, as I have said, the fullness of the mind. It simply cannot do its job without the mind.

The Sufi mystic Kabir Helminsky summarizes the relationship of the heart and mind in the following words.

> Beyond the limited analytic intellect is a vast realm of mind that includes psychic and extrasensory abilities, intuition, wisdom, a sense of unity, ascetic, qualitative and creative faculties, and

image-forming and symbolic capacities. Though these faculties are
many we give them a single name with some justification because
they are operating best when they are in concert. They comprise a
mind moreover in spontaneous connection with the cosmic mind.
This total mind we call heart.[6]

The heart can be the whole mind only when it includes *all* the
dimensions of the mind, even those that are normally ignored and
subsequently underdeveloped. Including these powerful means of
knowing and being allows the heart to fulfill its intended role as
an organ of spiritual perception. When combined with reason, it
offers us a trustworthy source of wisdom.

But trusting your heart is quite different from trusting your
emotions. The equation of the heart with emotions has done
much to trivialize our understanding of both the heart and emotions. In both Christianity and Islam, the heart has very little to
do with personal affectivity, passions, and feelings. As we have
seen, emotions have an important role to play in the fullness
of the mind because they are much more closely connected to
thoughts and other mental processes than we normally realize.
They do not represent a challenge to rationality but instead represent its complementary other half that holds the potential to
make the mind whole. For wholeness, all mental capacities need
to be brought down into the heart, where they can be woven together into a harmonious and cooperative alliance. This is what
the wisdom tradition means when it speaks of the heart as the
fullness of the mind.

We are so used to hearing the mind prattle on with a constant
stream of thoughts that we seldom give it our full, undivided attention. But when the heart speaks, everything is hushed. If we are
really listening to it and have come to trust it, we will immediately
recognize its authority and know that we can accept it as the final
word. And if the mind is aligned with the heart, all arguments
cease and the mind can finally rest.

The core of the transformational journey is aligning the heart and mind. The longest and hardest journey humans will ever take is the short distance from the head to the heart. Ultimately, all spiritual practices center on helping the mind enter and take up residence in the heart. Like a bird going back to its nest at the close of the day, the mind winds up all its activities as it settles into its home in the heart.

Helping the Mind Find Its Home in the Heart

Nothing arising from within the egoic self or the binary brain can be of any help in moving the mind down into the heart. As Einstein said, no problem can be solved from the same level of consciousness that created it. Typically, however, when we become frustrated by the smallness of our egoic self and tired of its petty games, the easiest thing to do is to use the tools at hand. If, for example, we determine that we would like to be less judgmental, we *try* to be less judgmental. Or if we feel exhausted by the effort demanded to keep up with the games of the false self, we *try* to fix the false self. But the will is at the core of these efforts to try to fix things that we think need fixing, and the will is a faculty of the ego. Our effort only strengthens the egoic self. This is the great problem with the self-improvement projects undertaken under the direction of the ego. They only reinforce the root of the problem.

Anything that feels like a default strategy in life always arises from the default egoic operating system. The ease with which we slip into these automatic ways of responding should be a warning signal to us that we are using the tools of the ego to attempt to transcend the limitations of ego.

The only tools that can help the mind find its way to its home in the heart are those that come from the heart. From the perspective of the mind, they seem utterly useless and totally trivial. What the heart offers is an invitation to let go and let be. It bids us to step back from the striving that has characterized our lives and risk, allowing our lives to emerge unshaped by our willful egoic manipulations. It encourages us to trust the divine coherence of life by releasing our attachment to our thoughts and daring to go to a much deeper center in our being. It invites us to surrender our inherent tendency to grasp and cling and, as a result, discover the gifts of being held and truly belonging. It challenges us to throw away the primitive handheld compasses we have fashioned with egoic tools and dare to depend on our inner magnetic compass of the heart. It assures us that the heart is so deeply and eternally resonant to our Source that it alone can guide us on our journey to alignment and wholeness.

Meditation and Heart-Shaped Becoming

While there may be other ways to replace the egoic self with the heart-shaped self, the one that has been most prized by the wisdom tradition—and the one I can recommend with the most confidence—is the practice of meditation, or, as it is commonly described in the Christian tradition, contemplation. This practice is the access key that allows us to download the upgraded operating system for the egoic self. It couldn't be designed better as a way to help the mind find its way back into the nest of the heart.

The unique leverage meditation offers in this transformational process comes from the fact that it engages the mind through the heart, not the ego. Rather than activating normal mental processes, it sidelines them. Rather than either using or trying to manage thoughts, it simply disregards them. And by doing so, it moves us to a place much deeper than thoughts. It shifts us into the region of the heart.

All forms of meditation pull the plug on the constant self-reflexive activity of the egoic mind by teaching us to detach

ourselves from thoughts. But this practice in detachment pays
dividends that extend far beyond thoughts.

The human heart has infinite spaciousness. However, each time
we cling to something, the heart's spaciousness is reduced. The
more we cling, the more the heart is constricted. And the more
things we cling to, the more chronic and life-strangling the con-
strictions become. Meditation addresses this by teaching us gentle
release of the things we are clinging to. This starts with thoughts,
but over time we get into the flow of release and begin to notice
other attachments that are strangling the heart and limiting freedom. One by one, we release them. Whatever we cling to we can
learn to hold lightly by practicing the simple action of release.
Doing so unblocks the clogged arteries of the spiritual heart and
lets life start to flow freely again through us.

Detachment involves learning to hold things lightly. Nonattachment isn't indifference or drifting through life without engagement but rather freedom from grasping and clinging—two
hallmarks of the ego. Grasping and clinging shut down the heart.
Detachment opens it up, and nonattachment keeps it open. The
detached heart is free to feel most fully, love most passionately,
and guide most dependably as we seek to translate concern into
constructive action.

Meditation opens up heart-shaped possibilities of becoming. It
introduces us to the spaciousness of the heart and gives us access
to its unique resources of wisdom, intelligence, and compassion.
It teaches us to see reality as it is, not as we normally perceive it
through the filters of egoic consciousness. It encourages us to let
things be as they are, not try to force them to be something the ego
thinks it needs. Slowly but surely, it enables us to see life through
oneness. Much more than merely having a mystical experience
of oneness, this is possessing the eyes of the heart, which makes
it possible to see larger wholes and find our place within them.

Unlike downloading a new operating system for a smartphone
or tablet, this download takes more than a few minutes. In truth,

it's not a totally new operating system but a totally transformed old one. Transformation is evolutionary, not revolutionary. It doesn't eliminate and replace; it reconstructs and re-forms.

But make no mistake about the fact that the changes are real. You will first notice them in your consciousness. You will begin to see differently as you shift from a preoccupation with uniqueness to a sense of amazement at connections and similarities. As you bypass categorization you will be struck by the larger whole that contains and supersedes all categories. You will also notice yourself moving beyond either/or to both/and, from grasping and clinging to the freedom to release all things. Increasingly, you will intuitively sense the harmony of the larger whole. In the depths of your being, you will begin to know the divine coherence of life and the way in which you and everything else belong within this wholeness. These changes are the firstfruits of what has classically been described as "unitive" or "non-dual" consciousness. But it is important to remember that these things are not achievements. They are gifts. You didn't engineer them. Your part was simply to access your heart; the rest unfolds as you continue to release the stranglehold that ego previously had on it.

Reading books about meditation might be interesting, but it will never be transformational. No one I know has ever experienced the sorts of changes I have just described while using the available tools of the egoic self—and believe me, I have had lots of practice trying to do so! It is the *practice* of meditation that is transformational. Don't worry about whether you have the technique right. That's an ego trip. Just meditate. Find a way that works for you and just do it—regularly and faithfully. To draw on an old joke, the way to replace the egoic self with the heart-shaped self is same way you get to Carnegie Hall—practice!

Make it a life practice, in all senses of this term. Recognize that you are doing it for the rest of your life, and allow it to become a lifestyle, not a fad spiritual diet. Treat it as a way to practice life. Meditation isn't preparation for life—it is life itself. Notice how you become aware of the fact that rather than meditation giving you a place to go *to*, it becomes the place you go *from*.[7] Your inner sanctuary begins to flow out into life, which is how it should be. It reflects the expansiveness of the heart. Never simply concerned with the private and personal, the human heart reaches out and wants to connect you to the living, pulsing heart of the universe. This is why the heart is at the core of all human becoming.

Cultivating Heartfulness

Don't settle for stillness or clarity of the mind as the goal of media-tion. Ultimately, what we need is purity of heart. Purity of heart is singleness of heart—to will one thing above all else. It is to love one thing above all else. It is to have your heart aligned with the pulsing heart of the universe and sufficiently open so that love can flow freely through it.

To some, this suggests that the goal of meditation should be understood as heartfulness, not simply mindfulness. But the dis-tinction between these two is more apparent than real. Buddhism clearly teaches that compassion is an expression of enlightenment; wisdom and compassion are so integrally related that neither can be fully present apart from the other. Likewise, Jesus taught that without love we have nothing; when the heart is right, everything else will reflect this fundamental alignment at the depths of our being.

But if the heart is the fullness of the mind, then heartfulness is impossible without the mind being fully present. We must bring heart *and* mind to life if we are to live with wisdom. And this is precisely what happens in true heartfulness.

I have a friend who ends every conversation or message to me by saying, "May your heart flow freely." Heartfulness isn't so much about being compassionate as allowing compassion to flow through us. It isn't so much about doing the loving thing as allowing love to flow through us. We all suffer from hardened arteries of the heart. We all experience blockage that restricts the freedom of the heart to be a conduit of love and compassion. Heartfulness is heart healthiness. Nothing could be more important for our personal well-being or the well-being of the world than humans having healthier hearts.

My own lack of deep compassion was one of the things that first got me seriously engaged in soul work. Those who were closest to me were in the best position to notice the gaps in my love. To those at a bit of a distance, my general niceness papered over the deficit. But by my early thirties, I was aware of how easily irritated I could be with certain people and how little empathy or compassion was present in my inner response to them. I was also keenly aware of the Great Commandment—to love God with all my heart and soul and strength and to love my neighbor as myself—and that I didn't love either God or others nearly as well as I loved myself.[8] But I longed to love both God and others more. I longed to have a heart of compassion, and I set about trying to figure out what was blocking me from doing this so that I could fix the problem.

It is not difficult to recognize the egoic way in which I attempted to correct a problem of the ego by trying to fix it with the tools of the ego—in my case, effort. This doesn't mean that the inner work had no value. It had a great deal of value because it allowed me to know myself more deeply. It also helped me to see the next steps I had to take to embrace and ultimately integrate the parts of me that had been eliminated from the false self I was busily trying to create. But it didn't make me more loving.

The movement into the next stage of my inner journey was not initiated by a felt need to fix something. I was ready to move beyond egoic fixing only after I finally and completely gave up on any further efforts to pull myself up by my psychological and spiritual bootstraps. I knew I was far from perfect, but by age forty, I had abandoned all efforts at self-improvement and was simply trying to live my life with depth, presence, and authenticity. That release from the pressure of all my self-improvement agendas felt tremendously freeing. It also expanded my awareness. I noticed that my feet were dangling in the river of becoming. I could feel the current as it gently flowed under, over, and around them. I wanted to wade into that stream of life and stop observing (and writing about!) it from the safety of the shore. Although this isn't always the case, for me there really was nothing holding me back. I had achieved enough to know how little my achievements ultimately mattered, and I felt that anything I had to lose would be lost by staying on shore rather than plunging into the flow of life. So that is what I did. I jumped into the deep end of the pool of contemplative practices, and I discovered that the pool was empty. But it was precisely this emptiness that created the space to help my mind sink into my heart. It was in that empty space that my heart began to align with the heart of the cosmic Christ, and my mind began to find its place within it.

While this journey is still far from over, I have come to know that love is at the center of it all. I sensed this when I wrote the following words in 2002, and since then I have come to know even more deeply just how true this is.

> In spite of the trivializing influence of romantic and sentimental views of love in Western culture, love is the strongest force in the universe. Gravity may hold planets in orbit and nuclear force may hold the atom together, but only love has the power to transform persons. Only love can soften a hard heart. Only love can renew trust after it has been shattered. Only love can inspire acts of genuine self-sacrifice. Only love can free us from the tyrannizing effects of fear.[9]

Life is all about love. Though the heart can't be reduced to love, the heart has no meaning apart from love. If a person is given everything the world can possibly offer, without love that person has absolutely nothing of value. Love is that important—that foundational to life itself.

Love at the Heart of Life

I t is one thing to say that the most important thing in human life is love. While this might seem to be a bit of a sentimental overstatement, the point is at least arguable. However, it is quite a jump beyond such an assertion to suggest that life itself—not just human life—is all about love. This implies that love has something to do with inanimate life, not just humanity. It might even suggest that love has something to do with the evolutionary unfolding of the cosmos.

There would be no reason to pay any attention to such a claim if it came from me. But it is worth paying attention when we hear this same assertion coming from the preeminent paleontologist, geologist, and cosmologist Teilhard de Chardin.[1] The two big themes of his life's work are that the fundamental thrust of evolution is whole-making, and that it is love that holds everything that is together. The first of these shaped the understanding of life as a series of nesting Russian dolls that I have already shared in earlier chapters. The second is our focus in this chapter, where we start by looking at the science that suggests that it is love that holds the universe together.

What's Love Got to Do with It?

It certainly does seem a bit strange to suggest that love holds every-thing together. But maybe *strange* is too gentle a word. Perhaps it sounds utterly preposterous to suggest that love holds atoms together, keeps planets in their orbit, or attaches us to the surface of the earth as we spin through space at 1,040 miles per hour!

There can be no doubt that a strong attractional force is at work in the universe and that this force forms the glue that holds things together at a physical level. Imagine the first moments after the Big Bang, when all the hot, molten bits of the matter that formed our proto-universe began to cool. Fragments are spread across millions of miles of space, and that distance increases second by second. But then—and this is the great surprise—the trillions upon trillions of atoms begin to move toward one another. Hydrogen atoms begin to clump with other hydrogen atoms and eventually fuse into helium atoms. Other atoms combine in different ways, but always, in response to some great force of cosmic attraction, part-wholes come together to form larger wholes. And so it has continued ever since.

The name we usually give to this force of cosmic allurement is gravity. Teilhard de Chardin called it love or, even more frequently, God-Omega. The concept of gravity only describes the attrac-tional force and doesn't accommodate the whole-making nature of evolution. Love encompasses both. It describes the attraction of physical bodies to each other, but it also takes account of the way in which this attraction draws parts together into larger wholes.

If love sounds like too personal a term, that's the point. Evo-lution, according to Teilhard de Chardin, is oriented toward the integral wholeness that is achieved through unity in love. Yearning for wholeness through love is at the heart of a deeply personal cosmos. Love is the awareness—at some level of consciousness—of belonging to another, the awareness of being part of a whole. But if consciousness itself is something shared (in some form or another) by everything within the cosmos, then perhaps the foundation of consciousness is this basic awareness of being held in and drawn forward by love.

Love is the deeply personal presence of the passionate force at the heart of the Big Bang universe, and it is the same passionate force at the heart of its continuing evolution. Love is the fire that breathes life into matter. It is the force that worked against entropy as elements groped their way toward union in love, and it is the force that continues to draw together and unite in ways that enhance differentiation. Many of us name the ultimate depth of this energy God, but whether we call it God or love, the name is not as important as the reality behind the name. Drawing together and unifying is the very nature of love. It is the nature of God. Love is the foundation of everything that exists.

Eros and Cosmic Longing

Sexuality obviously has an important place in this primal force of attraction. It also has an equally important role in whole-making. In the words of Teilhard de Chardin, "Everything in the universe is made by union and generation—by the coming together of elements that seek out one another, melt together by two, and are born again in a third."[2] The route to wholeness is through union that preserves differentiation. And the longing for union is eros.

Love-energy is intrinsically relational; union and the creation of more and larger wholes is its end. Sexual energy is the energy that comes from being sexed—that is, separated from the whole. Our longing for wholeness is intimately tied up with our sexuality.

Sometimes we are more aware of a longing for union, and sometimes we are more aware of a longing for wholeness. But the two
are one, and they come together in sexuality. We are wholes longing
for more wholeness, and somehow we intuit that the wholeness
we seek lies in union.

This same energy draws everything that exists toward wholeness
and completeness. Every atom, every cell, every plant or animal,
every planet and star—everything is pulled by the same primal
force of allurement toward the larger whole within which it belongs. Everything that exists is "sexed"—that is, cut off from the
larger whole and drawn toward it by the passionate, vitalizing
force of eros.

We ache in every cell of our bodies, aware at some level of
consciousness that we are little pieces of a larger whole. But this
ache is also a deep and fundamental source of energy. It is the
engine that drives everything else; it is our core longing and our
most basic source of energy. It is life surging through us, calling
us toward union that preserves differentiation.

Having sex is only part of sexuality. Much broader than its narrow genital expression, sexuality is the love-energy that propels us
toward intimacy, personalization, and wholeness. It seeks connections—not with strangers but with others who are experienced
as a part of our self.

Sexual intercourse is not essential for eros to lead us toward
wholeness and union. There is no question that, at its best, it can
provide a transitory experience of union and a peek at the larger
whole within which we belong; this is an important part of what
makes it so powerful. But the same erotic love-energy is at work
whenever we are led forward by attraction. The whole universe
is charged with eros, so it is not surprising that it bubbles up
and forms a part of all close relationships. Sexuality is simply
the body's awareness of aloneness and love-energy propelling the
body to do something to overcome it. Every step we take toward
doing so is fueled by eros.

The Relational Nature of Everything

If the whole universe is under the thrall of love-energy moving everything within it toward connections that express themselves in greater wholeness, then it is time to pound the last nail in the coffin of the Newtonian mechanical worldview. It is time to be clear about the fact that the universe is more like a choreographed but continuously evolving dance than a mechanical clock. Everything within the universe is evolving in ever-deepening patterns of interdependence.

Reality is inherently relational. Everything that exists dances within networks of connections and layers of attractional bonding. As expressed by the poet Wallace Stevens, "Nothing is itself taken alone. Things are because of interrelations or interactions."[3]

In her book *Relational Reality*, Charlene Spretnak reports that the picture of the physical universe provided by recent science matches exactly with what we now know about the human realm.[4] Everything and everyone is hitched to everything and everyone else. Everything that exists does so as part of a network of relationships. But even more important, everything and everyone is constituted by their relationships, both internal and external. In short, being is being in relationship. We are our relationships.

Take, for example, what we now know about the relationship of humans to their environment.[5] People working in buildings with daylight experience less illness and absenteeism than those working in artificial lighting. The picture is the same in terms of interpersonal relationships. People with many friends catch fewer colds and manage stress better than those who have few. As they age, people with many friends are less likely to develop dementia or experience decline in motor functions such as walking, gripping, and balancing. For people of all ages, even ten minutes of talking with someone each day, by phone or in person, boosts mental performance and emotional well-being. Increasing embeddedness in interpersonal relationships even has a significant and direct effect on the strength of the immune system. People with more friends are four times less likely to come down with a cold after receiving a direct injection of the virus! Perhaps, as Thich Nhat Hanh has suggested, existence is not so much a matter of being as inter-being. For human well-being, we seem to need real connections with both the natural world and the embodied presence of other people.

But if being is being in relationships, becoming is becoming even more deeply embedded in those relationships. It is offering our consent to the force of love as it seeks to draw us into life-nurturing relationships with our bodies, minds, souls, and spirits, as well as our environment, the earth, the cosmos, and all those who share it with us. When we fail to nurture relationships with those realities that exist beyond us, our becoming is stunted. But every time we offer our consent to the forces of love that seek to draw us into life-nurturing relationships, human and cosmic unfolding surges ahead. It is as simple as that.

Love and Transformation

Richard Rohr often says that the two classic paths toward transformation are the way of love and the way of suffering. Beyond these two major paths, there are as many minor routes to transformation as there are individuals. We each awaken in ways that are unique to us, and transformation starts with an awakening. Both great love and great suffering offer enormous potential for transformation—quite possibly the greatest potential of any experiences available to us. But as potentially powerful as these experiences are, most of us sleep through them and avoid the invitations that they offer to awaken us from our self-preoccupation so that we can leave our minds and come to our senses.

In general, anything that produces significant internal conflict, a disruption of meaning and self-coherence, or a sense that our way of being in the world needs to change has this potential to awaken us. Some of these experiences emerge from the circumstances of our lives—things like great love or great suffering—and some arise from entirely internal sources. I have known people who simply grew weary of living in the twilight and longed to emerge into the full light of day. I have known others who were driven to awakening by boredom with their lives. That was very much my own experience when I realized in my mid-thirties that the place of safety I had created within beliefs was protecting me from real knowing. I was experiencing life through the filter of my mind and realized that I longed to engage reality in a much more direct way. It was the start of what came to be a cascading series of awakenings for me.

Recently a young woman approached me seeking transformational coaching. She told me she had been on a transformational journey since adolescence and described for me some of the substantial changes she had experienced as she pushed herself out of her comfort zone and overcame her fears. It sounded like a classic tale of a self-made woman. But while her journey was far from insignificant, it was something quite different from authentic transformation. I asked about her inner journey, and she told me about how much she had learned about herself from confronting challenges in her life. I asked her what she had learned from suffering, and she told me that it had taught her that she needed to take charge of her life and quit sitting in passivity and helplessness. Then I asked one final question; I asked her what she had learned from love.

At this, her polished persona began to crack. She dabbed a tear in the corner of one eye, took a bit longer to answer, and then told me that she had just left her partner of five years. She said that this was a sensitive area for her. I asked if she could tell me about the relationship and why it ended. She said that as much as she loved him, she wasn't growing. As loving as he was, he wasn't challenging her to grow in the ways she needed. What this had taught her, she guessed, was that love could get in the way of transformation. This was why she had left him, and she would not quickly make this mistake again.

Love hadn't awakened her. Instead, the threat love presented to her well-ordered world led her to reject it. Love threatened— as it always will—her self-encapsulation and autonomous self-regulation. It invited surrender and compromise, and she quickly decided that these things had no place on the path she had chosen. Love seemed like a siren call from a dangerous shore, inviting her to the ruin that would come from having to give up the safety and coherence of the world she had created. She wanted nothing whatsoever to do with it.

The destabilization that she experienced through this encounter with love had the potential to awaken her and lead to genuine transformation. It produced the prerequisite significant internal conflict, disrupted her self-coherence and the sense of the meaning of her life, and challenged her way of being in the world. But as we all so often do, she responded to this disruption by choosing to run from it.

Neither love nor suffering automatically produces transformation, though both offer continuing opportunities to awaken. But love offers even more. Love offers opportunities to heal the wounds that keep us in a sort of cryptogenic deep freeze. It offers us a chance to decenter the ego. It offers us an opportunity to embrace parts of the self that have been previously rejected—particularly as we notice ourselves projecting them onto those we most deeply love. It offers us the chance to journey with another in such a way that calls forth who we really are. By doing these things, love offers us the chance to align with life and the developmental and evolutionary currents within it that are ultimately so much stronger than our pitiful attempts at dog-paddling in the river of life.

Love demands hospitality to the inevitable tensions or conflicts that are part of any intimate relationship. The more intimate the relationship, the more love presses these demands. If we dare to face rather than seek to escape them, these tensions give us a chance to wake up in the areas of life where we avoid naked, direct contact with reality. Intentionally embracing the challenges that are always present in a love relationship also gives us an opportunity to connect more deeply both with a partner and with life itself.

Love invites us to allow our energy to radiate outward rather than to congeal or be used for self-protection. It invites us to move from defensiveness to openness, to stay present and open to each other when we would rather attack or run and hide. Love alone is capable of completing our being as it joins us with others at our very depths and center.

Love is our true destiny. Thomas Merton writes, "We do not find the meaning of life by ourselves alone—we find it with an-other."[6] The meaning of our lives is revealed to us most clearly in love by the one we love. We will never be fully real until we lose our egocentric selves in love—either with another human person, with life, or with God. But this love requires that we "climb out of the cradle where everything is getting and grow up to the maturity of giving—without concern for getting anything in return."[7] Many people, including the woman I mentioned earlier in this chapter, simply find this demand too great.

Love is the glue of all personal connections. It is the source of the deepest wellsprings of human vitality. Love is the only hope for overcoming our isolation. "Nothing in creation is ever totally at home in itself," John O'Donohue says. "No thing is ultimately at one with itself."[8] Love offers the intimacy and deep belonging for which our souls ache. Nothing vitalizes the human spirit like the experience of a loving connection—something that assures us that we are not alone and that we count for something to someone.

Love is life reduced to its essence—an intensification of life that reflects its fullness and wholeness. It is for love that we came into the world, both to experience this communion and self-transcen-dence and then to pass it on to others. We do not become fully

only love links us w. life

human until we give ourselves away to others in love—not only in sexual love but in mutual care, creativity, and spiritual concern.

Love becomes the luminous and transformational presence of God when we relinquish the need to control both our lives and the lives of others. Ilia Delio writes, "It creates personality in us not by adding anything special but by chiseling away the stuff we smother out our lives with, as if we could become something other than ourselves."[9]

Love really is the strongest, most creative, and most generative and regenerative force in the universe.

What the World Needs Now

Given the potency of love for healing, growth, and transformation, what could possibly be more important for the world than humans learning to give and receive love? The love we need to learn to give and receive, however, is not the soft, sentimental kind of love associated with Valentine's Day but the hard, unflinching kind associated with loving those who will not or cannot return our love.

Love has become a transaction rather than a gift. But the only love that can ever be transformational is love that is given away, not exchanged. The only love that can ever truly make us and others whole is the love we give and receive as a surprise, even to ourselves.

But notice that I speak of giving and receiving love—not receiving and then giving. Love has not only become a commodity of transaction, but it has also become something we have come to believe we must store up and pass on only after our own supplies are at a high enough level to warrant the risk of depletion. We think that the love we have to give to others is the excess of what we have received and hoarded. But this misses the whole point of love.

Love is like a stream: it is meant to flow. Once you block the flow, it begins to go stagnant. Love that is hoarded is no longer life-enhancing. It quickly becomes toxic. Wounds don't heal by soaking in love but by passing love on.

Hoarding love always means that at least two people lose. The person who hoards love loses it because it is in the giving of love, not simply the receiving of it, that life is nurtured. And the person who was deprived of love because someone else hoarded and didn't pass it on to him or her is robbed of the chance to pass love on to others.

The world's great spiritual teachers have always challenged us to do exactly this. Jesus taught by word and example to love one's enemies, not just one's friends. He was clear that love given in exchange—that is, given so it will be given back—is not love at all.[10] Love that is not freely given is not love at all. The Dalai Lama's teachings on compassion give the same message. If you want to be happy, look for every opportunity you can find to be compassionate to those whose paths cross yours.[11] If you want to make the world a better place for yourself and others, keep the flow of love going.

The world community desperately needs more of us to learn how to be agents of compassion. The Charter for Compassion that grew out of Karen Armstrong's 2008 TED talk seeks to help this happen.[12] It presents us with a simple statement and a bold vision.

> The principle of compassion lies at the heart of all religious, ethical and spiritual traditions, calling us always to treat all others as we wish to be treated ourselves. Compassion impels us to work tirelessly to alleviate the suffering of our fellow creatures, to dethrone ourselves from the centre of our world and put another there, and to honour the inviolable sanctity of every single human being, treating everybody, without exception, with absolute justice, equity and respect.
>
> It is also necessary in both public and private life to refrain consistently and empathically from inflicting pain. To act or speak violently out of spite, chauvinism, or self-interest, to impoverish, exploit or deny basic rights to anybody, and to incite hatred by denigrating others—even our enemies—is a denial of our common

humanity. We acknowledge that we have failed to live compassionately and that some have even increased the sum of human misery in the name of religion.

We therefore call upon all men and women to restore compassion to the centre of morality and religion—to return to the ancient principle that any interpretation of scripture that breeds violence, hatred or disdain is illegitimate—to ensure that youth are given accurate and respectful information about other traditions, religions and cultures—to encourage a positive appreciation of cultural and religious diversity—to cultivate an informed empathy with the suffering of all human beings—even those regarded as enemies.

We urgently need to make compassion a clear, luminous and dynamic force in our polarized world. Rooted in a principled determination to transcend selfishness, compassion can break down political, dogmatic, ideological and religious boundaries. Born of our deep interdependence, compassion is essential to human relationships and to a fulfilled humanity. It is the path to enlightenment, and indispensable to the creation of a just economy and a peaceful global community.[13]

The growing number of individuals, churches and faith communities, cities, and even countries around the world that have adopted this statement and pledged to work toward making their communities places of compassion is an encouraging sign. It really is the only hope for our world.

Our challenge is to trust the power of love enough to place it at the very heart of our lives as individuals and communities. We should allow ourselves to be seized by love and lose ourselves in love and then pass this liberating and whole-making contagion on to others. And we should help others to see the importance of doing the same, in both their individual and communal lives. Our challenge is, in the words of Ilia Delio, "to create ways for love to evolve into a global wholeness of unity, compassion, justice, and peacemaking."[14]

8

Living Wholeness

Now that we have a more concrete idea of what it means to allow love to flow through our lives, it is time to return to the theme of wholeness and look more carefully at what wholeness actually looks like. What does it mean to be whole and live out of this place of wholeness? How do we find our way into the larger wholes within which we already exist? And how can we make this a living reality not just in our lives but also in our world?

These are some of the questions I will explore in this chapter. Before I do, let me quickly identify three well-traveled paths that superficially seem to lead to wholeness but actually only strengthen the egoic self, deepen our fragmentation, and increase our alienation from the self, others, and the world. I think it is important to clearly identify these broad roads if we are to find our way to the narrow, less-traveled paths to wholeness.

Well-Traveled Roads to Be Avoided

The three paths I have in mind are individualism, tribalism, and perfectionism. All are deeply rooted in popular culture. Worse yet, the tragic collusion of contemporary Christian culture with popular culture only heightens their potency and danger. Within these paths you may not always hear talk of fulfillment or wholeness, but that is what they promise.

What they deliver is much less and quite different. They deliver safety and places of belonging that imperil people's journeys toward authentic fullness of being. I write of these three well-traveled roads because I have spent time on each of them. I know their seductive powers from personal experience.

Individualism

The roots of individualism are, of course, much deeper than contemporary culture. They are the roots of modernity itself. But they have come to play a particularly dangerous role in the West where, if there is one defining characteristic of culture, it is individualism.

Psychologist Martin Seligman describes the core problem with the rampant individualism we now experience. "In the past quarter-century," he writes, "events occurred that so weakened our commitment to larger entities as to leave us almost naked before the ordinary assaults of life. . . . Where can one now turn for identity, for purpose, and for hope? When we need spiritual furniture, we look around and see that all the comfortable leather sofas and stuffed chairs have been removed and all that's left to sit on is a small, frail folding chair: the self."[1]

The self is too small, partial, and vulnerable to withstand the assaults of life alone. It was never meant to do so. It was meant to exist within a web of interdependence that provides substance and belonging. Lacking this, it secures pseudo-substance through egocentrism. Everything becomes about me—my goals, my needs, my plans, and my fulfillment. The woman I described in chapter 7 who backed away from love because of the way it threatened to compromise the actualization of her fullest potential is a good example of this, but the path she was on is so common that you can easily supply your own examples. Self-fulfillment is not wholeness. Neither is it completeness or fullness of being. It is a pitifully poor substitute; it is egocentric self-encapsulation.

Tribalism

Another way in which we compromise the discovery of our belonging and completeness is by allowing our identities and belonging to crystallize around our tribe. Belonging to a tribe is not the issue. We all exist within families, communities, socioeconomic groups, nations, and countless other groups, but tribalism is something different from that. Tribalism is identity defined by exclusion and fueled by mistrust, suspicion, and at least latent hostility.

When I was growing up, my tribe went to church in a building that did everything it could to not look like a church. It wasn't even called a church; it was called a Gospel Hall. Halfway up the block from us was a Baptist church in a building that was recognizably religious (despite the absence of a cross), and just beyond that was an imposing Roman Catholic cathedral sitting at the top of the hill in all its typically Romanesque architectural grandeur. Just around the corner were the meeting places of two other major tribes in our town—the Presbyterians and the Anglicans. What was interesting was not the large number of churches for a small town or that they all clustered together but that the tribal identities associated with each were so strong that in school everyone knew who belonged to which tribe—or worse, who wasn't part of any of them! More tragic than that, I was taught that those in my tribe were the true Christians—a designation that intentionally excluded members of the other churches as well as everyone else.

Exclusivism is one of the hallmarks of the tribal path to belonging and identity. Loyalty is always first and foremost to the tribe, and clear, impermeable boundaries are maintained by clear distinctions between "us" and "them"—with strong negative feelings

churchism

toward "them." These negative feelings are the veneer for the latent hostility toward outsiders that is never far below the surface. Racism is a particularly clear example of virulent tribalism, though it simply illustrates its essential dynamics.

Tribalism is a path toward belonging that gets stuck at a primitive level. While it involves more belonging than the path of egocentric individualism, and while it can potentially form a way station on the path to larger wholes and the belonging they provide, a person is usually forced to leave the tribe to do so. This seriously limits the possibilities of transformation, which demands owning all the parts of one's story. It also sets the person up for a life of dis-identification rather than expanding identifications, this being the doorway to authentic transformation.

Perfectionism

I have already talked about perfectionism and how different it is from wholeness in chapter 1, so I don't need to spend much time on it now. It too is another broad, well-traveled road that takes us in a direction quite different from an authentic path of living wholeness.

Many of us know something of the temptation represented by this path. And if we take it we quickly discover that it is a path of quicksand; it suffocates and does not deliver what it promises. Holiness as sinless perfection is a religious face of perfectionism that is equally dangerous. When we stop confusing holiness with morality and instead understand perfection as purity of heart and a singleness of identity and consciousness that grows around this, we can begin to see how holiness and wholeness are simply two faces of the same coin.

Whether perfectionism takes this religious expression or a nonreligious one, it builds on the egocentric individualism of the first false path. It is pursued as an individual accomplishment—the result of *my* discipline, *my* asceticism, and *my* hard work. It is a path that arises from our small ego-selves and tightens the cords around us that keep us there.

Less-Traveled Paths to Be Trusted

The road to wholeness is actually more of a path or a trail. This has important implications for walking it.

I am an avid hiker and am painfully familiar with the fact that while trailheads can usually be identified without too much difficulty, trails themselves are typically much less clearly marked. The hiker often encounters points where the trail divides, and it is unclear which path to take. But there is no need for worry with the trails I am going to describe. The pathways to wholeness are all woven together. Go far enough on any of them, and you will always be invited to branch out and take a parallel trail that allows other parts of you to be woven into the fabric of wholeness that you truly are. Each pathway includes all of the others. While they appear separate, they are simply parts of the pathway of living wholeness. As with roads leading to Rome, all of these paths can be counted on to lead to deeper fullness of being and becoming.

If you are attentive, your heart will clearly let you know whether the path you are traveling is leading to wholeness. It will also lead you to the best trailhead for launching the next phase of your journey. As I describe several of these interweaving paths, don't worry about where to start. Start where you are, and follow your heart.

Expanding Ways of Accessing Wisdom

As surprising as it might sound, *how* we make judgments and decisions has an important impact on whether consciousness evolves. Living out of the wisdom associated with our present pool of knowledge, opinions, and decision making leaves both consciousness and identity in a static place. Expanding our ways of accessing wisdom increases our inner openness and puts us on a path that enhances transformational becoming.

I know many people who are quite content with the pool of wisdom they access within their mind and their communities. They have no interest in listening to other voices and other perspectives because they feel they already have a corner on the market when it comes to truth. Dialogue is of no interest as they cling to their beliefs. It is no wonder that they are threatened by any encounter that could potentially change them. I understand how these people feel, but I also feel the sort of sadness for them that I feel for anyone who has the opportunity for fuller development and more authentic living but turns away because of fear.

Many of us, however, have learned the enormous value of voices and perspectives other than the ones most familiar to us. Perhaps you already know something of the way in which other voices help you to better understand your own beliefs and perspectives. And perhaps you know the richness of meeting others in their difference and uniqueness, not just their sameness. Genuine encounters with people in other religious and spiritual traditions provide great joy. When we dip into the great sea that I have been calling the perennial wisdom tradition, that is what we receive.

How exactly do we do this? My advice is not to settle for books. Knowledge is seldom transformational, but authentic encounter—which is much more personal than the acquisition of information—holds enormous, life-changing potential.

Earlier I said that the wisdom tradition is a living tradition, which is why it is best accessed in people, not books. But where do we find it? Start with friends or acquaintances who deeply live a tradition that is different from yours. Take one of them out for lunch, and tell that person you really want to better understand his or her culture and religious tradition. If you can't identify anyone in your circle of acquaintances, look for interfaith organizations in your community for ways to learn firsthand about the wisdom of other faith traditions, but be prepared to make this part of an ongoing practice, not simply a one-time visit. Don't simply seek information; seek wisdom and the expanded inner horizons that come from accessing it in new ways and places.

I have long found engagement with indigenous people to be a great way of getting in touch with deep streams of wisdom. Regardless of where they are in the world, the belief and meaning systems of indigenous people bear deep similarities to one another and to the big concepts that I have been discussing in this book. A Maori anthropologist friend of mine tells me that the very notion of an indigenous person who is living his or her traditional culture but who does not believe in the connectedness of all things is unimaginable. Most indigenous languages do not have a word for spirituality, but their way of living will usually be deeply spiritual and deeply resonant with the teachings of the perennial wisdom tradition. Do yourself a great favor and cultivate a friendship with at least one indigenous person. Allow that person to lead you into his or her world, and I guarantee it will lead you to experience new depths in your own.

Learning to attend to your heart is also an important way of accessing wisdom because, as I have already noted, the heart is the fullness of the mind. As such, the heart lets us access a greater intelligence than we can tap simply through reason. The cultivation of the subtle faculties of intuition and attention to the heart's resonance and alignment are, therefore, critical paths to walk as we open ourselves to the possibilities of the sort of changes in consciousness and identity that I have described as transformation.

The practices of sensing heart resonance and attending to intuitions are more subjective than relying on reason alone. It is important to have an objective context to help in our interpretation of heart data. While the heart does have an inner authority, it must be aligned with the external authority of tradition. Whether we recognize it or not, we have all been deeply influenced by the traditions and cultures of our childhood. Though we may consider it irrelevant, the tradition of our formation is something we need to engage deeply if we are to transcend it.

A very close friend of mine who was raised a nominal Christian but spent several years studying to be a Buddhist monk in Southeast Asia was told by a wise teacher that he needed to connect deeply to his own tradition before he could advance on the spiritual journey. My friend didn't think of himself as Christian, but he followed his teacher's advice, and in the process of a thirty-day Ignatian spiritual exercises retreat encountered Christ in a way that won his heart—even as he continues to speak of Buddha having won his mind.[2]

Your tradition isn't the same as your beliefs or practices. It is the context that shaped those beliefs and practices and within which your worldview was developed. Only when we have engaged our own tradition deeply, critically, and honestly can we truly engage another tradition. This was the wisdom that my friend's teacher recognized and displayed.

Without a tradition, we cannot progress very far in accessing or living wisdom. Apart from living out our journey within a tradition, we remain spiritual dilettantes who explore a variety of expressions of spirituality but never face the hard lessons that come with commitment to one path and the other people sharing it. Many people who were formerly religious undertake this journey of pick-and-choose spirituality, but the path it involves quickly degrades into egocentric individualism.

My own religious lineage has included being fundamentalist, evangelical, Reformed, and now Anglican—more specifically, the Anglo-Catholic subtradition of Anglicanism. My spiritual lineage has been more stable. For the past thirty-five years it has been the Christian contemplative tradition. Together, these have provided the framework within which I have interpreted the Bible and the subjective stirrings of my heart.

Identifying and embracing your lineage is an important part of any pathway to greater wholeness because it involves remembering your own story. All the parts of your journey must be woven together if you are to transcend your present organization and level of consciousness. For myself, the great challenge was reembracing traditions that I have grown beyond and that offered—even at the time—an oppressively small worldview. I did not want to be an exevangelical or an exfundamentalist. Too many people live that life of dis-identification, and I did not want to share their anger and "stuckness." It was essential, therefore, for me to identify and embrace the gifts that had come to me from these traditions. This was the way in which I came to truly know that everything in my life belongs, that every part of my story has made important contributions to who I am. And the same is true for you.

To sum up, expanding the ways that we access wisdom puts us squarely on the path of further becoming in several important ways. First, it decenters our egos and confronts us with other ways of being in the world. It also presents us with larger vistas and other perspectives and worldviews; when we engage these while at the same time deeply living our own tradition, the result is usually a deepening of our understanding of and engagement with our own tradition. After twenty years of extensive engagement in interfaith and intercultural dialogue, I am more deeply Christian than I have ever been.

Most important, supplementing head knowledge with heart knowledge expands consciousness and allows us to access a broader and deeper intelligence. Invariably, where consciousness goes, identity follows. As both consciousness and identity begin to shift, we find ourselves engaging with life from a different, higher platform—a platform from which we can see farther and clearer.

The pathways I have described directly contribute to transformation by deepening our engagement with our own story. They invite us to remember and reembrace our story, and the integration that results from this process is an important part of wholeness.

Living with Inclusiveness

A second and closely related pathway involves living with increasing inclusiveness. The egoic tendency to divide and simplify

120 Human Being and Becoming

is foundational to its binary nature. It is, however, tremendously destructive to not only our souls but also our societies and world. Every time we identify with "us" against "them," we vilify the other and set them up as a scapegoat. Since the basic mechanism of scapegoating is projection—that is, the unconscious way of dealing with things we are unwilling to acknowledge in ourselves—we project those parts of ourselves onto others so that we can hate both those parts and the other person. This pattern of exporting our unwanted parts of self and then righteously hating them in others is a fundamental dynamic of the egoic self. But it is tremendously dangerous because it is the root of violence.

Whenever we exclude things from ourselves and project them onto others, we then must exclude those people from "us" and depersonalize as "them." On one side of this boundary is everyone we judge to be "us" and onto whom, therefore, we project our ego ideal. All others serve as containers for the projection of everything we reject in ourselves. We may disguise and even repress the hatred we feel for them (that's what good socialization teaches us), but it will always be present in at least a latent form. This is the reason exclusiveness is so dangerous.

The alternative is to live with ever-expanding boundaries of inclusiveness, which involves moving from loving *myself* as myself to loving *us* as myself and finally to loving *all of us* as myself. It involves moving from identifying with my tribe to identifying with humankind and all of creation.

This is a pathway, not an accomplishment. The goal is not to like everyone. The way to get onto this pathway is simply to allow yourself to encounter everyone you meet as a "thou" rather than an "it." Martin Buber reminds us that every "it" can become a "thou," or better still, every "it" is already a "thou" whom we can learn to recognize and honor.[3] Meet and engage everyone with the generosity of empathy, and you will find it quite easy to recognize them as a part of the human tribe of which you are simply one member.

All those you reject as worthy of being met as a "thou"—and believe me, that is what you do when you engage them as an impersonal "it"—wounds both you and them in the same way. Treating another as less than human degrades both your humanity and theirs. However, the simple act of inclusiveness affirms both your humanity and theirs.

Don't be quick to conclude that you already live this way. Take a mental walk through your day and notice how you relate to the homeless, to people of ethnic groups you grew up thinking of as inferior, to those of political or religious persuasions different from your own, to those of gender or sexual orientations different from yours, and to those of a different age and demographic or socioeconomic class. Even more simply, notice those who bother you the most and with whom you have the least patience. That is where inclusiveness must start.

Think about organizations to which you belong that practice exclusiveness, which you support by your participation in them. Inclusive living has no boundaries. Everyone is treated with the same respect and dignity simply because they are human. Sound naive? That's the voice of your ego speaking. Dare to challenge it by committing yourself to walk the pathway of inclusive living. It may challenge your club memberships and affiliations (religious or otherwise), but wholeness isn't a project of the individual self. It will always have a communal expression. This doesn't excuse you from taking the steps on the path that you alone can take, but don't forget that we walk with others on this path. *Whom* we are walking with will unquestionably influence the extent of our inclusiveness—and therefore the extent of our wholeness.

Learning, Growing, and Serving Together

The next pathway to wholeness has already been discussed, but I want to identify it separately here to be sure we do not miss its importance—namely, that we must be prepared to intentionally walk this pathway of wholeness *with others*. I say intentionally because it is an inescapable fact that we cannot pass through life without others. We are interconnected whether we want to acknowledge that reality or not. Living out of wholeness and walking a pathway of deepening wholeness involves intentionality, not simply passing through life on automatic pilot.

At least three dimensions of the communal nature of the journey of becoming are worth noting: learning, growing, and serving. The place where this journey usually begins is learning with others. Because we remain individuals within the larger wholes of our belonging, it is natural that we continue to learn as individuals. *Our* journeys will always also involve *my* journey because "I" remain an integral part-whole within the larger whole of the "we." Therefore, our continuing openness to personal growth is important, although personal growth isn't the same as self-improvement. Personal growth does not involve fixing things about ourselves that we do not like. It involves nurturing development. Sometimes this must start with healing. And because our wounds almost always arise within an interpersonal context, so too must our healing. We must heal with the help of others and in relationships with others, not simply by curling up in our cave of our selves and trying to engineer our own healing.

Learning *with* others starts with learning *from* others. Personhood is a gift we receive from others; it isn't an individual achievement. And growth into fullness of personhood happens as we journey with others.

A few years ago a good friend of mine decided that he no longer considered himself to be a Christian. After decades of church involvement, he felt that since he no longer believed the creeds, the time had come to resign his membership and spend his Sundays in better ways. I asked him whether there was anything he would miss. He said that his one worry about finally giving up on church was that he might stop growing.

Despite the many things that made my friend dislike church, the one thing it had dependably given him over the years was, he said, an opportunity to reflect on his life. Although he didn't usually agree with the answers given by the church to the important questions it addressed, his involvement kept him honest because it confronted his natural tendency to associate only with people who shared his opinions and values.

Whatever else growing together means, it certainly includes the fact that real involvement with real people—particularly with the assorted ages, ethnicities, personalities, and political and sexual orientations that one encounters in a healthy community—will always give us opportunities to grow in ways that we cannot by succumbing to the individualism of our culture. Of course we can find these opportunities for growth in other relational contexts, not just churches, but commitment to journeying with others within a community offers important advantages over merely hanging out with friends. We don't get to choose the other people in a community. Instinctively, we tend to avoid those who fall outside our natural comfort zone. But once we commit ourselves to journeying and growing together, those people in our community that we might never choose as friends offer us a chance to deal with the precise issues we need to confront if we are to become whole.

Learning together and growing together should also translate into serving together. Community should be the place in which we discover and are affirmed in our calling—that is, the way of serving that is rooted in our uniqueness but takes its form as our gifts and passions meet the great needs of the world. Living our calling is where we discover the meaning of our life and how we find our fulfillment. Both of these things happen best in the context of journeys that are intimately shared with others. In this we become part of a larger whole in its most dynamic sense— a whole that is not simply a nest of belonging but a powerful context for serving.

Holding Beliefs with Humility

Beliefs are a lot like barbed wire. They divide us from others and keep us separate. And yet beliefs seem to be an unavoidable result of how our brains work as they attempt to make sense of the world. In terms of whether beliefs support becoming, the crucial issue is how we hold them.

The egoic way of holding beliefs is to wrap our identity around them. Ego says, "I *am* my beliefs." This means we treasure our beliefs, polish them, trot them out whenever we need to distinguish ourselves from others, and defend them when we feel threatened. But used in these ways, beliefs are little more than psychosocial constructions. They are the way we cobble together an identity that sets us apart from others we do not identify with. We think our beliefs are the fruit of hard personal work exploring life's big questions, but under the influence of ego we ask only questions for which our beliefs already provide pat answers.

When we hold beliefs in this way, their primary function is to protect our fragile egos from the threat of truly encountering those with other beliefs. Holding beliefs by wrapping our identity around them sets up clear boundaries between "us" and "them," with beliefs forming the barbed wire fence that defines the boundary. The reason I add the barbed wire to the fence is because of the way in which beliefs held in this way are always tinged with hostility. Under the guise of being clear, what we really want is separation from those who hold wrong beliefs—a separation fueled not only by defensiveness but also hostility. If this premise seems doubtful, consider the fundamentalists of any religious tribe.

But this is not the only way to hold beliefs. Heart-shaped becoming involves holding beliefs with humility. We *have* beliefs—just like we have thoughts, opinions, and ideas—but we are not reducible to any of them. Understood in this way, beliefs are no longer a sword with which we do battle with those who see the world differently than we do. They express some of what we see from the vantage point of engaging the world from the platform on which we presently stand. They reflect our culture and convictions. But they are not us. And we are not them.

I am quite aware that some people feel threatened by the very suggestion of holding their beliefs with humility. They fear that this involves altogether too much distance between them and their essential self. They fear that this distance might lead them to lose their moral compass, which might cause them to descend into the base instincts of their animal nature. But ultimately this fear is not theirs; it is the fear of the ego. As the ego is tamed under the influence of the journey toward heart-shaped wholeness, the threat will lessen, and freedom will increase.

Rather than dividing us from others, beliefs held with humility allow us to encounter others in a deep and nondefensive way. Now we can afford to get to know those with whom we journey in a deep way, and they can feel safe enough to do the same with us. The way in which our beliefs are held makes all the difference!

Characteristics of Living Wholeness

The harmony of the universe is based on wholeness that retains differentiation. Without wholeness we hear only the cacophonous noise of the various parts of the self clanging together. But without differentiation, we hear only the pure sound of a single tone and not its harmonics.

Many people who go to see the leaning tower of Pisa miss the really astounding experience offered by Pisa, Italy. The Baptistery that sits adjacent to the famous tower has such superlative acoustics that several times each day someone with a singularly pure voice enters it, hushes the awaiting crowd, and then sings a single note. Instead of hearing only the isolated E that is being sung, the acoustics of this incredible space allow those in it to hear the subtle over- and undertones of the surrounding C and G that make it a harmonious, whole chord.

All of life is filled with these harmonics of wholeness. Unfortunately, we seldom hear them.

How do you know whether you are on a path that involves living out of wholeness and that leads to increasing wholeness? You will hear harmony, not simply the cacophony that is familiar to a fragmented self. You will sense the energy of the larger whole, an energy that goes beyond your own. You will, at least occasionally, experience the thrill of being simply a small part of a large cause—of being a tool seized by a strong hand and put to an excellent use. You will be comforted in knowing that we are all interconnected. In a very real sense, therefore, what you do for another, you do for yourself. Love passed on to others becomes the most meaningful form of self-love. Care of the earth and its inhabitants becomes care of self.

We live wholeness when we re-member our individual stories—embracing each part of them and allowing them all to be woven together into the whole we are becoming—and through them experience a deeper sense of being part of a greater whole. We live wholeness when we know we belong—to people, to a place, to a community and tribe, to earth, to God (however named), and to the cosmos. We live wholeness when we feel a deep sense of responsibility to live generatively by helping those younger than we are—and those not yet born—to live well. We live wholeness when we know that what we already have is enough; all we need is to be resourceful with it.

Living wholeness is participating in the dynamism of love that gathers everything together into greater unity and consciousness. It is living with openness of mind and heart, encountering others not as strangers but as parts of our self. When we enter into the heart of love in this way, we enter the field of relatedness and come to know our truest and deepest belonging and calling.

Wholeness and love are inseparable. Love leads to larger wholes, as there is no true wholeness that is not built on love. In the words of Ilia Dileo, "Our challenge today is to trust the power of love at the heart of life, to let ourselves be seized by love, to create and invent ways for love to evolve into a global wholeness of unity, compassion, justice and peacemaking."[4] This is living wholeness and love.

Epilogue

THE FURTHER REACHES OF WHOLENESS

In my discussion of the Great Nest of Being in chapter 2, I suggested that everything that exists is spread across five levels of existence—matter, life, mind, soul, and spirit. But everything that exists came from spirit and completes its journey of becoming by returning to spirit. This does not mean, however, that anything is left behind in our transformational journey. Our return to our origins in spirit (or, in more traditional Christian language, in God) never leaves soul, mind, life, or matter behind. Development is based on envelopment. Becoming does not mean abandoning lower levels of existence but rather no longer being limited to them. Integration always precedes transformation, and so as our journey takes us into the further reaches of becoming, we bring matter, life, mind, and soul already woven tightly together.

Spirit is the goal of the entire sequence of this journey toward wholeness. All of life is flowing in this direction. The Christian Scriptures tell us that even matter groans as it waits for its wholeness.[1] It is hard to imagine how matter fully reconnected to spirit will look or behave differently, but that is the way in which all things are being restored to their fullness in Christ. All of life participates in this groaning. All of life flows in this same river of becoming that draws us back to our source. This means that we and everything else that exists are being drawn toward the fullness of matter that is infused with life, which is infused with mind, which is infused with soul, which is infused with spirit. Weaving all these things together is what Christians refer to as "salvation" or "redemption." But this is not simply an individual matter; it is the big-picture story of everything.

Spirit calls us to become more than we are when we have settled for small places of belonging. It urges us to find our true home in relationship to the self-transcendent. A life aligned with this transcendent reference point allows us to soar in realms unimaginably broader than anything encountered when our selves are organized around our souls, minds, or bodies. The journey of spirit leads us toward transcending our small, cramped, lives. It leads us toward the spaciousness of the true self—a self that knows its place within larger wholes. And it leads toward a corresponding expansion of consciousness in which our seeing and knowing arise from places of wholeness, harmony, and belonging.

Because spirit is not a possession but a participation in the transcendent whole that is God, it always orients us toward this spiritual horizon. Every step of the journey of human becoming is spiritual because the flow of life leads back toward the transcendent ground of our existence. However, as we focus on the more advanced stages of human becoming, the spiritual nature of the journey becomes more and more obvious. It is also more difficult to describe apart from the language of religion. While I tried in earlier chapters to speak first and foremost as a human, I must now make more use of the language of my tradition—Christianity—to describe the way in which matter, life, mind, soul, and spirit are fully reconnected. Others can use the language of their tradition, but it is futile to attempt to describe these further reaches of becoming without employing the concepts of religion. The language of generic spirituality is just not up to the task.

The Spirit-Centered Life

To describe the higher stages of this journey as movement toward a spirit-centered life is to say that not only are all the levels of existence being woven together but also the dynamic center of the person is spirit. Let me be clear what I mean by *spirit*. As I noted earlier in an endnote, I have *not* been following the frequently adopted custom of Christians to capitalize *spirit* to distinguish the spirit of God and the spirit of humans. This is not to say that humans are the same as God but simply to acknowledge that, in the words of Cynthia Bourgeault, "As we move toward our center, our own being and the divine being become more and more mysteriously interwoven."[2] This is the testimony of the mystics of all religions and spiritual traditions. They identify the center of their knowing (consciousness) and being (identity) as their oneness in love with their divine source—a source that Christians name as God.

This is not pantheism—the belief that the universe is identical with God. It is more appropriately described as pan*en*theism—the belief that God both interpenetrates every part of the natural world and at the same time transcends it. Christian mystics do not think that they are God. They know that in union with God, human personality is neither lost nor converted into divine personality. Even though we may sink into what Meister Eckhart speaks of as the Divine essence, we never *become* that Divine essence.[3]

Another dimension of this union with the spirit of God is that it also involves a union with everything. Because everything that exists is held in the unity that is Christ, everything that exists is one in Christ.[4] The old joke about the mystic who walks up to the hotdog vendor and says, "Make me one with everything," misses the point. We are already one with everything. What's missing is awareness—the gift that is ours when the spirit-centered life is a reality of consciousness and identity, not merely a belief.

This oneness is not simply an experience. It starts with awareness that the apparent separateness of the one from the many is an illusion. It is consciousness of the reality that both the one and the many are held together in God. The experience of oneness emerges out of this awareness and becomes a stable part of consciousness.

The medieval Flemish mystic John of Ruysbroeck describes this knowing of the self as one with everything as being based in our knowing of our self as existing in God. "All creatures," he notes, "are immanent in this unity, and if they were to be separated from God, they would be annihilated, and would become nothing."[5] This is not merely some arcane point of theology. It is a reality that can be known when we see through spiritual eyes, reminding us that it is not just the mind that is enlightened on this journey of awakening but also the heart. If we are to see God, we must see not simply through the eyes of the mind but also the eyes of the heart.

To be one with everything is to recognize the illusory nature of our separateness. We establish boundaries to try to reinforce individuality, but what we get is isolation and alienation. We distinguish between the natural world and ourselves, and as a consequence we exploit the environment from which we feel estranged. We think we are separate from other people, but as a result we lose awareness of our underlying shared humanity. Boundaries disrupt the flow of participative energy between elements of creation that can be distinguished but are intimately interrelated. To realize that we are already one with everything is to participate in the very life and being of God.

Love in the Spirit-Centered Life

The spirit-centered life is meaningless apart from love. Those who know and live this life the fullest are those who talk about it as love-inebriated. Hafiz, the fourteenth-century Sufi mystic, is a good example. He wrote volumes of love poems to and about God that were filled with passion and sexual imagery. Consider just one, titled "You Better Start Kissing Me."

> Throw away
> All your begging bowls at God's door,
> For I have heard the Beloved
> Prefers sweet threatening shouts,
> Something in the order of:
> "Hey, Beloved,
> My heart is a raging volcano
> Of love for you!
> You better start kissing me—
> Or Else!"[6]

Christianity has an equally strong sense of the union with God being in and through love. Consider a poetic conversation between Mechthild of Magdeburg, the thirteenth-century Christian mystic, and her Divine Lover.

> "God, you are my lover,
> My longing,
> My flowing stream,
> My sun,
> And I am your reflection."

God answers,

> "It is my nature that makes me love you often,
> For I am love itself.
> It is my longing that makes me love you intensely,
> For I yearn to be loved from the heart.
> It is my eternity that makes me love you long,
> For I have no end."[7]

Ursula King describes the story of the Christian mystics as an "all-consuming, passionate love affair between human beings and God."[8] They speak of a burning desire for the presence of their Beloved and an unquenchable desire to know the depths of God for humankind. They know that the path of becoming is a path of learning love.

Love is the way to know God, and it is through eyes of love that we see, know, and participate in the wholeness that is God. Love is the way we overcome the illusion of our separateness and the way we are drawn into union with God. Love is the way ego is dethroned. Love really is at the heart of everything that has life and is becoming.

We cannot truly see the natural world as a creational outpouring of Divine love and not begin to care for it. Similarly, we cannot see others through the eyes of God without our hearts opening and love flowing with renewed vigor. As we live in God and increasingly see others through eyes of love, we discover that the ways in which we normally categorize people and set ourselves apart from others are less and less meaningful. While distinctions can be made, they are a distraction because they take our attention from the much more fundamental sameness that arises from oneness. When we focus on the distinctions, we miss the fact that the other person is both a face of ourselves and a face of Christ. We also miss the common journey that we share as humans who dare to follow spirit on the journey of human awakening and unfolding. We miss the fact that we are all children of God.[9]

Barriers to Becoming

What could be strong enough to make us want to hold back from walking this path of love-saturated becoming? Why do we both long for participation in the wholeness and love that is our source and destiny and at the same time resist it?

For most people, the answer to both questions seems to come down to fear—fear of losing control, fear of the unknown, fear of the judgment of those in our spiritual community, and fear of stepping off the platform on which we presently stand before we have our feet firmly planted somewhere else. We fear that after stepping off that platform we may face a free fall. But the only way to know that we are safe in making this transition into a more spacious state of being is to take that step.

Taking this step requires trust in that which is beyond the self. Transcendence always requires a relationship to the self-transcendent, and if we are to step off the platform on which we presently stand without being firmly planted on where we hope to land, this relationship must be characterized by faith that is expressed in trust. We cannot pull ourselves up to higher levels of becoming by our own bootstraps. Genuine transformation always involves trusting consent to the flow of the stream that surges through life. Knowing that this flow is from and returning to God helps many of us with that trust.

Some of those for whom this trust is difficult have been taught that life flows away from God. Obviously this makes it harder for these people to trust anything other than specifically safe and religious things, such as spiritual practices taught by their tradition and their tradition's interpretation of the Bible. These people become threatened by the sorts of things I have been saying in this book and are extremely unlikely to have read it to this point. They are the ones who send me angry messages denouncing me as a heretic.

But you have gotten this far. Something in what I am saying speaks to deep places within you—places that long for deeper and fuller becoming. Don't be distracted by your fears. Listen only to your longings. They come from your heart. Listening to them will deepen your relationship with your heart.

Follow your heart. It will lead you to the deeper life you seek. It has for me and for many, many others. The path is trustworthy. Even though at times you may doubt it, you won't be walking it alone, and don't attempt to. Watch for others who are walking this path and connect with them.[10] Doing so will give you a great introduction to the larger whole within which you belong!

Notes

Introduction: An Invitation to an Incredible Adventure

1. Pierre Teilhard de Chardin was a French philosopher and Jesuit priest who trained as a paleontologist and geologist and subsequently took part in the discovery of Peking Man. I won't often be referring directly to his work, but his writing, particularly *The Phenomenon of Man* (New York: Harper & Row, 1961), has been a major influence on my thinking about human being and becoming.

2. I will have more to say about the perennial wisdom tradition as I proceed, but at this point let me simply describe it as a summary of the timeless truths about the nature of the self, the world, ultimate reality, and God that appear in the world's major religious traditions. In his book *The Perennial Philosophy: An Interpretation of the Great Mystics, East and West* (New York: Harper Perennial Modern Classics, 2009), Aldous Huxley describes it as, "The metaphysic that recognizes a divine Reality substantial to the world of things and lives and minds; the psychology that finds in the soul something similar to, or even identical with, divine Reality; and the ethic that places man's final end in the knowledge of the immanent and transcendent Ground of all being" (vii). For a fine series of recent articles on the perennial wisdom tradition, including a helpful discussion of its relevance to Christianity, see "The Perennial Tradition," *Oneing* 1, no. 1 (Spring 2013).

3. See, e.g., Brian Thomas Swimme, *The Hidden Heart of the Cosmos* (Maryknoll, NY: Orbis, 1996); Ilia Delio, *The Wholeness of Being* (Maryknoll, NY: Orbis, 2013).

4. Using more traditional language, St. Irenaeus spoke not of Being but of God. In what follows I will use this same traditional language from time to time but will often refer to the one who in the Hebrew Bible self-identified as "I AM" (Exod. 3:14) by terms such as Being, the Ground of Being, or other capitalized words.

Chapter 1 Being Human

1. The idea of loving others as our self is found in almost identical form in the sacred texts of Hinduism, Jainism, Buddhism, Zoroastrianism, Judiasm, Christianity, Islam, and Sikhism. For details, see Mary Pat Fisher, *Religion in the Twenty-First Century* (London: Routledge, 1999), 104.

2. The wisdom tradition is best understood as a living tradition, not a compendium of wise words. The life of the tradition is wisdom teachers who do not simply communicate propositions but also draw on the tradition to encourage and facilitate personal transformation. Cynthia Bourgeault, a widely recognized wisdom teacher, notes that the hallmark of their teaching is "their use of pithy sayings, puzzles, and parables rather than prophetic pronouncements or divine decree. They spoke to people in the language that the people spoke, the language of story rather than law" (Bourgeault, *The Wisdom Jesus: Transforming Heart and Mind—A New Perspective on Christ and His Message* [Boston: Shambhala, 2008], 23). Bourgeault notes that when this teaching method is combined with the content and focus of Jesus's teaching, it is clear that he was first and foremost a wisdom teacher belonging to the Jewish branch of the Near Eastern wisdom tradition known as *mashal*.

3. First articulated by the ancient Greek philosophers (primarily Parmenides, Plato, and Aristotle), the understanding of these three transcendentals strongly influenced Augustine, Aquinas, and other Christian theologians who grounded being in the nature of God. As God created out of the Divine self, being was then shared with humans and everything else that existed, making clear the fundamental connection between all that had being with Being itself.

4. Genesis 1:10–25.

5. Richard Rohr, *Yes, and . . .* (Cincinnati: Franciscan Media, 2013), 384.

6. Reported by President Barack Obama in his words of public condolence on the death of Nelson Mandela, December 5, 2013.

7. Leonard Cohen, "Anthem," in *The Future*, Columbia Records, 1992, www.azlyrics.com/lyrics/leonardcohen/anthem.html.

8. Although contemporary authors often capitalize the first letter of *spirit* when they wish to refer to God (something I myself have often done), I will not be doing that in this book because it introduces an unhelpful distinction between the human and divine spirit. In the words of Cynthia Bourgeault in *Centering Prayer and Inner Awakening* (Cambridge, MA: Cowley, 2004), 13, "As we move toward center, our own being and the divine being become more and more mysteriously interwoven." Spirit, I believe, is the element that does the interweaving.

9. Rohr, *Yes, and . . .* , 374.

10. Henri J. M. Nouwen, *The Wounded Healer: Ministry in Contemporary Society* (New York: Doubleday, 1972).

11. A very helpful discussion of the heart from the perspective of the wisdom tradition can be found in Cynthia Bourgeault, *The Wisdom Way of Knowing: Reclaiming an Ancient Tradition to Awaken the Heart* (San Francisco: Jossey-Bass, 2003).

12. Genesis 3.

13. Ken Wilber, *Integral Spirituality* (Boston: Integral Books, 2007).

Chapter 2 Cosmic Interconnectedness

1. This fragment from John Donne is worth quoting in its entirety: "No man is an island, entire of itself; every man is a piece of the continent, a part of the main." It is drawn from *Devotions upon Emergent Occasions* (1623), "Meditation XVII."

2. David Foot famously claimed that demography explains two-thirds of everything—whether that "everything" is the stock market, education needs, health patterns, or trends in housing, recreation, or social behavior. See David Foot, *Boom, Bust, and Echo: How to Profit from the Coming Demographic Shift* (Toronto: Footwork, 2004).

3. The dates for demographic generations are debated, but in the West baby boomers are generally considered to have been born between 1946 and 1964; generation X is associated with birth dates between 1965 and the early 1980s; generation Y, or millennials, between the early 1980s and early 2000s; and generation Z from the early 2000s to the present. Earlier cohorts have been given names, but much less attention has been paid to their characteristic behaviors and values.

4. Arising out of ideas developed by Plato and Aristotle but heavily influenced by Augustinian and Thomistic Christian theology, the notion of a great chain of being was a way to understand the relationship of matter to God, breaking this down into a hierarchically ordered range of forms or levels of reality. Its roots go back to ancient Egyptian and Greek civilizations, although it is continuous through ancient Chinese thought, Hinduism, Judaism, Buddhism, Christianity, and Islam.

5. This foundational insight of the perennial wisdom tradition has now been confirmed by modern science. Since Einstein, we know that matter is condensed energy. Matter and spirit are not, therefore, fundamentally different; spirit is simply a more subtle form of energy. The three levels between matter and spirit—life, mind, and soul—are all forms of energy that can be placed between matter and spirit in terms of the density of energy that they represent. At this point, science may recognize only matter and energy, but eventually it will discover that energy is simply the condensation of consciousness, i.e., of spirit. See Valentin Tomberg, *Meditations on the Tarot: A Journey into Christian Hermeticism*, trans. Robert Powell (New York: Tarcher/Putnam, 2002), for helpful further discussion of these matters.

6. Quoted by Ken Wilber, *Integral Spirituality* (Boston: Integral Books, 2007).

7. Genesis 2:7.

8. James Hillman, *Re-visioning Psychology* (New York: Harper & Row, 1975), 3–50.

9. Karl Rahner builds this into the very heart of his theology with the dynamic impulse of God's creative power. He suggests that matter comes from spirit and develops "out of its own inner being in the directions of spirit" (Rahner, "Christology within an Evolutionary View of the World," in *Theological Investigations* [London: Darton, Longman and Todd, 1966], 5:164). This spirit-directed return to its source occurs under and through this process of self-transcendence, and matter ultimately returns to spirit.

10. Ibid. See also Denis Edwards, *Jesus and the Cosmos* (Eugene, OR: Wipf and Stock, 1991).

11. Paul Davies, *The Cosmic Blueprint: New Discoveries in Nature's Ability to Order the Universe* (West Conshohocken, PA: Templeton, 2004).

12. For a more comprehensive discussion of these stages of consciousness and identity and what's involved as a person moves from one level of organization to another, see David G. Benner, *Spirituality and the Awakening Self* (Grand Rapids: Brazos, 2012).

13. Evolution does not, of course, operate primarily at the level of the individual. These human evolutionary dynamics reveal themselves in only very partial ways in any particular person. Sometimes they may seem to be nonexistent. Nevertheless, each and every human is a member of the human community and a part of the cosmos that, as the larger wholes within which they exist, are increasing in complexity, consciousness, and wholeness even if these processes appear to have been unsuccessful in drawing a particular individual further toward his or her destined wholeness.

14. In no religion are these truths clearer or more foundational than in Christianity. God has been in the business of connecting spirit and matter since the first moments of the Big Bang. This was the beginning of the divine self being poured out into creation, the beginning of the transformation of spirit into matter that Christians call the incarnation. God's interest in the material world did not begin with a rescue plan for humans who had fallen into sin. It was from eternity an expression of spirit creating, infusing, and then sustaining matter so that matter could eventually return to its place of belonging within spirit.

Chapter 3 Meaning-Making

1. Etty Hillesum, *An Interrupted Life: The Diaries 1941–1943, and Letters from Westbrook* (New York: Henry Holt, 1996).

2. Nelson Mandela, *Long Walk to Freedom* (Boston: Little, Brown, 1994), 544.

3. Jelaluddin Rumi, *Rumi: Selected Poems*, trans. C. Barks (Baltimore: Penguin, 2004), 109.

4. My brother, Colin James Benner, was born on April 27, 1951, and died on January 18, 2014.

5. Richard Rohr, *The Naked Now: Learning to See as the Mystics See* (New York: Crossroad, 2009), 46–50.

6. Dag Hammarksjöld, *Markings* (New York: Alfred A. Knopf, 1966), 205.

7. John Sanford, ed., *Fritz Künkel: Selected Writings* (New York: Paulist, 1984).

8. Mandela, *Long Walk to Freedom.*

9. This fact was communicated by Robert Shrire, a personal friend of Nelson Mandela, in a lecture on Mandela's role in the making of postapartheid South Africa in Maputo, Mozambique, on January 2, 2014.

10. The aboriginal peoples of the West are a great exception to this statement. They remain very close to the perennial wisdom tradition. A close look at the worldview of the indigenous people anywhere in the world reveals that their worldview (which forms their implicit spirituality) is deeply grounded in the broad contours of the wisdom tradition.

Chapter 4 Mysteries of Personhood

1. While this quotation is widely attributed to Tenzin Gyatso, the fourteenth Dalai Lama, I have been unable to verify this citation or identify the source of the quotation.

2. For more on my understanding of and approach to dreams, see appendix 1 of David G. Benner, *Spirituality and the Awakening Self* (Grand Rapids: Brazos, 2012).

3. Depth psychology is the psychological tradition that was first mapped by Sigmund Freud and Carl Jung and continues to be explored by those who climbed on their shoulders and have thus been able to see even further into the depths of the human soul.

4. The same point is equally true in relation to the two hemispheres of the cerebral cortex and the complementary roles they play as parts of the whole brain. See Robert Ornstein, *The Right Mind: Making Sense of the Hemispheres* (New York: Houghton Mifflin Harcourt, 1991), for a further discussion of their respective contributions.

5. Antonio Damasio, *Descartes' Error: Emotion, Reason and the Human Brain* (New York: Penguin, 2005).

6. Total freedom of decision making at the first use of a drug like crack cocaine is actually quite unlikely, since openness to trying it would be influenced by previous drug history, among many other factors. However, the point of the illustration remains valid even if the freedom at the onset is not 100 percent. Clearly, whatever number is assigned at the point of first use would be higher than the number assigned at the tenth use.

7. For a summary of data related to twentieth-century democide collected by Professor R. J. Rummel, emeritus professor of political science, University of Hawaii, see www.hawaii.edu/powerkills/20TH.HTM.

8. See Ernest Becker, *The Denial of Death* (New York: Simon & Schuster, 1973) and idem, *The Denial of Death* (New York: The Free Press, 1975).

Chapter 5 Ego-Based Being

1. Genesis 2:7.

2. Eva Wong, trans., *Cultivating Stillness: A Taoist Manual for Transforming Body and Mind* (Boston: Shambhala, 1992), 35.

3. Quoted in Marina Warner, *Monuments and Maidens: The Allegory of the Female Form* (Berkeley: University of California Press, 2001), 189.

4. Abraham Maslow, *Religion, Values, and Peak Experiences* (New York: Penguin, 1994).

5. For more on cosmic consciousness as a level of consciousness, see David G. Benner, *Spirituality and the Awakening Self* (Grand Rapids: Brazos, 2012).

6. For further discussion of the relationships of egocentricity, ego, and self, see David G. Benner, *Soulful Spirituality: Becoming Deeply Alive and Fully Human* (Grand Rapids: Brazos, 2011).

7. As incredible as it may sound, Dr. Suzana Herculano-Houzel, a Brazilian neuroscientist, recently developed a method to count the neurons in a number of human brains, and the resulting average was 86 billion. See Azevedo et al., "Equal Numbers of Neuronal and Non-Neuronal Cells Make the Human Brain an Isometrically Scaled-Up Primate Brain," *Journal of Comparative Neurology* (2009): 513, 532–41. A more popular account of her work can be found at www.theguardian.com/science /blog/2012/feb/28/how-many-neurons-human-brain.

8. Describing the way in which the mind is initially organized as a default operating system is to resort to a computer analogy. However, since consciousness is

not simply a product of the brain, and since the brain is not simply a computer, this analogy is obviously imperfect. Despite these limitations, it can, I think, still help us to understand how this default level of consciousness works.

9. Neurologists Andrew Newberg and Eugene D'Aquili were the first to document the binary operator as one of the two fundamental cognitive systems within the human brain. See Andrew Newberg, Eugene D'Aquili, and Vince Rause, *Why God Won't Go Away: Brain Science and the Biology of Belief* (New York: Ballantine, 1991).

Chapter 6 Heart-Based Becoming

1. For the nonspecialist in heart science (or what is often called neurocardiology), a good and quite accessible overview of research in this area is provided by *The Institute for HeartMath*, a nonprofit institution devoted to the understanding and promotion of the alignment of the human heart and mind. Since *HeartMath* is both a research and an educational institute, the science it presents is cutting edge, and original research reports are easily accessible from its website. It can be found at www.heartmath.org/.

2. Matthew 6:21, 45; Luke 2:19.

3. Matthew 5:8.

4. Quoted in Whitall N. Perry, *A Treasury of Traditional Wisdom* (San Francisco: Harper & Row, 1986), 819.

5. Quoted in ibid., 491.

6. Kabir Edmund Helminsky, *Living Presence: A Sufi Way to Mindfulness and the Essential Self* (New York: Jeremy P. Tarcher/Putnam, 1992), 142.

7. Cynthia Bourgeault, *Centering Prayer and Inner Awakening* (Cambridge, MA: Cowley, 2004), 17.

8. Matthew 22:35–40.

9. David G. Benner, *Surrender to Love* (Downers Grove, IL: InterVarsity, 2003), 10.

Chapter 7 Love at the Heart of Life

1. In addition to *The Phenomenon of Man*, the books by Teilhard de Chardin that are most relevant to the things I discuss in this chapter are *Science and Christ* (New York: Harper & Row, 1968), and *The Divine Milieu* (New York: Harper & Row, 1960). One of the foremost interpreters of de Chardin's work, Ilia Delio, has also been a great help in my understanding of the role of love in de Chardin's cosmology, particularly her books *Christ in Evolution* (Maryknoll, NY: Orbis, 2008), and *The Wholeness of Being* (Maryknoll, NY: Orbis, 2013).

2. Pierre Teilhard de Chardin, *Writings in Time of War* (New York: Harper & Row, 1967), 191.

3. Wallace Stevens, *Opus Posthumous* (New York: Vintage, 1989), 189.

4. Charlene Spretnak, *Relational Reality: New Discoveries of Interrelatedness That Are Transforming the Modern World* (Topsham, ME: Green Horizons, 2011).

5. Drawn from research summarized in ibid., 12–15.

6. Thomas Merton, *Love and Living* (New York: Houghton Mifflin Harcourt, 2002), 27.

7. Ibid., 34.

8. John O'Donohue, *Eternal Echoes: Celtic Reflections on Our Yearning to Belong* (New York: HarperCollins, 1999), xxii.

9. Delio, *Wholeness of Being*, 186.

10. Luke 14:1–14.

11. "Compassion and the Individual," accessed June 2, 2015, Office of His Holiness the Fourteenth Dalai Lama official website, www.dalailama.com/messages /compassion.

12. charterforcompassion.org.

13. charterforcompassion.org/charter-karen-armstrong.

14. Delio, *Wholeness of Being*, xxv.

Chapter 8 Living Wholeness

1. Martin Seligman, *Learned Optimism*, abridged ed. (New York: Simon & Schuster, 2011), 284.

2. I tell more of the story of my friend Dr. Donald Woodside in a blog post, which can be found at www.drdavidgbenner.ca/meditation-and-contemplative-prayer -an-interview.

3. Martin Buber, *I and Thou*, trans. R. Gregory Smith, 2nd ed. (Edinburgh: T&T Clark, 1958), 25.

4. Ilia Delio, *The Wholeness of Being* (Maryknoll, NY: Orbis, 2013), xxv.

Epilogue: The Further Reaches of Wholeness

1. Romans 8:21–22.

2. Cynthia Bourgeault, *Centering Prayer and Inner Awakening* (Cambridge, MA: Cowley, 2004), 13.

3. William Ralph Inge, *Light, Life and Love: Selections from the German Mystics of the Middle Ages* (London: Methuen, 1904), Kindle location 562–65.

4. Colossians 1:15–17.

5. Inge, *Light, Life and Love*, 1768–71.

6. Daniel Ladinsky, *I Heard God Laughing: Renderings of Hafiz* (Oakland, CA: Dharma, 1996), 77.

7. Fiona Bowie, ed., *Beguine Spirituality*, trans. Oliver Davies (New York: Crossroad, 1990), 55–56.

8. Ursula King, *Christian Mystics: Their Lives and Legacies* (Crestwood, NY: St. Vladimir's Seminary Press, 2001), 4.

9. Acts 17:23–29.

10. An increasing number of people find these connections with companions on the journey online. Check out my Facebook page (www.facebook.com/DrDavidG Benner), Twitter account (www.twitter.com/drdavidgbenner), and website (www .DrDavidGBenner.ca) if you are looking for places where some of us congregate. Online communities are far from ideal as a replacement for face-to-face communities, but after committing the last few years to developing these cyberspace communities, I am astounded as to how meaningful they can be—either as a supplement or as one's primary spiritual community.

Index